JAN BRAAI SAYS ...

1. If you're in any doubt as to whe[ther] enough, then your fire is not bi[g...]

2. Wealthy urban and poor rural people all braai with wood – it's the great equaliser.

3. For my recipes you need three measurement tools: cups, tots and teaspoons. A tot glass is that same little glass they serve shots from in pubs. Even in the middle of nowhere, you should be able to guess with reasonable accuracy the size of a cup, a tot and a teaspoon.

4. If you think the meat is ready to come off the fire, then take it off. It's probably ready and busy drying out.

5. Eat smaller portions of better quality meat. If you can afford meat, and if you can afford this book, then you're probably not starving.

6. With a selection or combination of salt, pepper, garlic, olive oil, soy sauce, mustard, chilli, paprika, lemon juice, a fresh herb and a cold drink, you can braai a great meal with any cut of meat.

7. The fire you make after you've braaied is called an atmosfire.

8. Life's too short to peel potatoes.

Red Hot
JanBraai

This book is dedicated to the millions of South Africans who celebrate National Braai Day on 24 September every year.

In National Braai Day, we South Africans have a realistic opportunity to entrench a national day of celebration for our country, within our lifetimes. I believe that having a national day of celebration can play a significant role in nation-building and social cohesion as the observance of our shared heritage can truly bind us together.

In Africa, a fire is the traditional place of gathering. I urge you to get together with your friends and family around a fire on 24 September every year to celebrate our heritage, share stories and pass on traditions. Please help me spread that word!

Red Hot

JanBraai

BOOK**STORM**

MACMILLAN

CONTENTS

SOME WARM-UP THOUGHTS

I once met a man who was unimpressed that I braaied things like boerewors and sosaties. He believed it's not a real braai unless you're braaing a solid piece of meat, big enough not to fall through the holes of your grid. As you work through this book you'll notice I don't share that view. I feel quite strongly that everything tastes better when you braai it.

THIS IS MY SECOND BOOK

Yes, there is another book out there called *Jan Braai – Fireworks*. That was my first book and this is my second one so don't get confused. This book should be read as an extension of the first. Obviously you will be able to read, enjoy and prepare meals from this book without ever reading *Fireworks* but if you want to be properly educated in the art of braaing, read both. See *Fireworks* as the first half and *Red Hot* as the second half of a greater encyclopaedia on this fine and ancient art. The only recipe that is duplicated from *Fireworks* is that of *Roosterkoek* (page 160). This is because there are so many recipes in this book that should or could be served with fresh *roosterkoek*, I thought it would make life easier for you if we just included it in this book again for easy reference. At the time of writing this book you're holding, *Jan Braai – Fireworks* had already been reprinted a few times and, naturally, the publisher has committed to continue printing it as long as the public continues to buy it. It goes without saying that if you do not enjoy this book, I strongly advise you not to buy *Fireworks* as the same person wrote it in a very similar style.

WARNING: THIS BOOK REQUIRES THE USE OF COMMON SENSE

I want to apologise in advance to those surprised or disappointed by this, but you'll have to use your common sense and sound judgement when working your way through this book. Some of the statements I make are written like fact when they are clearly opinion. Most recipes are actually a matter of opinion. When I say, for example, that you need to add four cloves of garlic, that is not really a fact. If you like garlic, add more. If you don't like garlic, add less. Braai recipes are a bit like ash, neither black nor white but rather various shades of grey. If a recipe calls for red wine and you only have white wine available, use it. If it calls for rump steak and you prefer sirloin, use that. If it says serves four and you are six people, then it will probably feed you just fine, in slightly smaller portions and with some extra bread or rice. Similarly, if I say it feeds eight but you have the front row of the local rugby club over for dinner, clearly no matter how much meat you braai, it will serve three. On the following pages are some more specific examples of instances at the braai when I expect you to use your common sense.

Jan Braai

KEEP IN MIND ...

A 'TOT' MEANS A SHOT GLASS AND HOLDS 25 ML

I strongly believe in making life simpler rather than more complicated, for example the measuring system in my recipes: a cup (250 ml), a tot glass (25 ml) and a teaspoon (5 ml). Calibrate them by using water to check that five teaspoons go into a tot and that ten tots go into a cup. When the measuring cup, tot glass or measuring teaspoon is full but flat as it is when you fill it with liquid, it contains the given volume. If a recipe calls for half a cup just fill the cup or glass halfway. A tot glass is that same glass they serve shots from in pubs and in South Africa that is 25 ml. I think that even if you are braaing somewhere without them, you'll still be able to guess to a fair degree of accuracy how big a cup, a tot and a teaspoon are.

SAFETY ISSUES

Braaing is a fun activity and you can have a cavalier approach to adding things like garlic and chilli; but stick to some basic health rules:

- Wash your hands well before you start preparing and handling the food.

- Keep meat that is marinating in a fridge. Use non-reactive bowls for marinating meat. These can be glass, plastic or stainless steel and should have lids. We call them 'marinating bowls' in the recipes.

- Don't use marinade with raw meat juices in it as a sauce – either boil it first or paint it onto the meat before the last 5 minutes of braaing time so it has a chance to cook too. In the same vein, do not put braaied meat into the same container that held your raw meat before the braai.

THICKENING OF SAUCES, STEWS AND POTJIES

In a perfect world you'd never need to use a thickener. You would always have enough time and the ideal heat control to cook meat and vegetables till they are done,

with just enough liquid to ensure that nothing burns. The liquid would be reduced just right, forming thick rich gravy in your potjie at the exact time the meat is tender yet before it's overcooked. In real life it doesn't work like that though. In this book you will come across many recipes for meals prepared in potjies that contain liquid or sauce. Sometimes you'll need to add more liquid (like water) than indicated in the recipe as, for whatever reason (usually a hotter fire or a less tight fitting lid), your meal is simply drier and closer to burning than it should be. In other cases you'll end up with a sauce that is too runny or a bit too watery. Try one of the following ways to get the consistency of sauce thicker and more like gravy in a potjie (be it a traditional potjie or a curry):

1. Sprinkle some flour over the meat at the beginning of the recipe, then fry it in oil/butter before you add the liquid – which in this book is usually water, wine or stock.

2. Add some raw diced or grated potato at the beginning of the recipe – a starchy vegetable that will help to thicken the sauce as it cooks away.

3. Reduce the liquid until it is the required consistency. This means you simply continue to cook the meal uncovered until enough water has evaporated and you are happy with the consistency. Remember that this will also concentrate the flavours so first reduce then add salt afterwards.

4. Stir in some cornflour mixed with a little water at the end of the cooking process, and let the sauce bubble a while until it has thickened. This is a very easy option that works almost instantly. The technique is mentioned a few times in this book but please, even when cornflour is one of the ingredients of a recipe, and mixing it in is one of the steps, don't do it if you're already happy with the consistency of the sauce. Then just ignore that ingredient and step. The cornflour will not add anything to the taste of the meal; it will simply thicken the sauce, so only use when necessary.

Remember that most meals thicken a bit on standing so you want to rather finish cooking it when it's still a little runny, not when it's already a little dry.

ADDING SALT TO YOUR MEAL

It's a very good idea to follow my suggestion in many of the recipes and 'add salt to taste'. This means you take a spoon, taste the meal, and add a little extra salt if you feel it needs more salt. When in doubt as to how much salt, rather add less than more. You can just place some salt on the table when you serve the meal, and everyone can make the final adjustment to the salt level in their food themselves. Once you've added too much salt, it is a very difficult process to reverse. It's like trying to get toothpaste back into the tube.

These days, we are very fortunate with the ever-increasing variety and quality of salt available in South Africa, with local producers putting some quality products on the market. The cost of one packet of high quality salt is completely negligible compared to the cost of all the meat you will eat with that salt. In my opinion, using cheap salt is completely silly. At the braai fire you can use salt in a grinder, and at the table I like to serve salt flakes, both for taste and texture.

TOMATOES

One of the single biggest challenges our country faces foodwise is the lack of great tomatoes. Too many tomatoes sold in South Africa are not red enough but rather 'light pink with a touch of green', do not taste enough like tomato but more like water. So, when using tomatoes in potjies, you'll need to add some canned tomatoes or tomato paste.

In this book I specify cans of tomatoes as 'whole cherry', 'whole peeled', and 'chopped'. I prefer them in that order but you can use any of those options in any of the recipes irrespective of the one I specify in the recipe. The difference in result will be negligible.

MEASURING THE INTERNAL TEMPERATURE OF MEAT

In many of the recipes in this book I suggest braaing times but they can and will fluctuate due to factors such as: meat thickness, size of the fire, type of wood used, length of time you waited to start braaing after the fire was burnt out, wind speed and direction, and the height of the grid.

The length of time you braai the meat for is vitally important though, as the juiciness of the meat depends mainly on the final internal temperature of your meat. This means that the more 'done' you braai your meat, the drier it will be. Essentially you need to braai meat to exactly the point at which it is ready to be eaten and no more. To measure the internal temperature of your meat you need a 'digital instant-read food thermometer' and this is available at most speciality kitchen shops. The braai-equipment shelf of many supermarkets and outdoor shops also sell digital meat thermometers.

RECOMMENDED INTERNAL TEMPERATURE FOR MEAT TYPES

	Degrees Celsius (°C) in thickest part	Doneness
Beef	55–57	medium rare
Lamb	60–63	medium rare
Pork	70	medium
Chicken	77	done

POTJIES

WHAT TO BUY

The most common cast-iron pot is the classic-shaped, three-legged potjie. As it comes with three legs attached to its body, it's the most stable in a fireplace, as the others still need to be balanced on a separate stand or tripod. Start off by buying a size 3 of this pot. My classic shape size 3 potjie is the first potjie I owned in my life. It's the actual potjie on the cover of this book and I've had it since I was 19 years old (it was a birthday present). The second type of potjie you need in your arsenal is the flat-bottomed bake pot. Coincidently that is the second potjie that I owned in my life. This potjie is extremely versatile as you can both cook as well as bake stuff in it. Due to its shape it travels very well in the boot of your car, and when there is a hurricane outside you can also use it on a normal kitchen stove. I suggest you start off by buying a size 10 of this one. This potjie is smaller and easier to handle. When cooking mains for four people I always use this potjie, irrespective of the dish I am making. It's also absolutely perfect for making malva pudding in (page 188). As these are my favourite potjies, it should come as no surprise that for most potjie recipes in this book you need one of the two.

TREATING A NEWLY PURCHASED POTJIE

A potjie is made from cast iron. As such, there are some unsavoury elements inside your new pot upon purchase.

Cooking food in a brand-new potjie is a very bad idea as the food will not only look funny (it will have an unnatural dark colour even though you haven't burnt it) but it will also taste like iron. Preparing your new potjie is a very important yet simple procedure. The first step is to wash and scrub it properly using warm water, dishwashing liquid and steel wool. Dry it and then completely coat the inside with cooking oil (cheap sunflower oil will do the trick). Heat the pot until the oil begins to smoke and then wipe it clean with a paper towel. Repeat this oil, heat and wiping drill until the paper towel comes out clean. Now wash the pot and test whether it's ready by cooking *stywepap* in it (page 174). If the porridge comes out white and tastes fine, your pot is ready for general use.

POTJIE MAINTENANCE

Wash your potjie using warm water, dishwashing liquid and steel wool. Dry it well afterwards and store it with lots of crumpled old newspapers stuffed inside it. The paper will absorb moisture and keep it from rusting too badly. If it does show a bit of rust, just wash and scrub it off. Rinse the pot before using it and if you have not used it for a while, wash it. Some people coat their potjies with cooking oil during storage to guard against rust but that oil becomes a bit sticky and disgusting after a while so I steer away from it. If you go that route, wash the potjie properly before every use.

THE MAN-OVEN

Man-oven is my collective term for those outdoor cooking devices that are powered by a charcoal fire, where you mostly cook with indirect heat, and where the food is usually baked with the lid closed. You typically use a man-oven to braai larger cuts of meat or whole chickens. The most widely used man-ovens in South Africa are the kettle braai type. Personally though, I prefer the superior Kamado-style grills made from ceramic. Thanks to its ceramic shell, it has high efficiency, excellent insulation and the ability to accurately hold very high and very low temperatures for a prolonged period of time. Why would you need to accurately hold low temperatures for prolonged periods of time? To braai non-traditional large cuts like pork belly and beef brisket of course. See www.monolithbraai.co.za for more details.

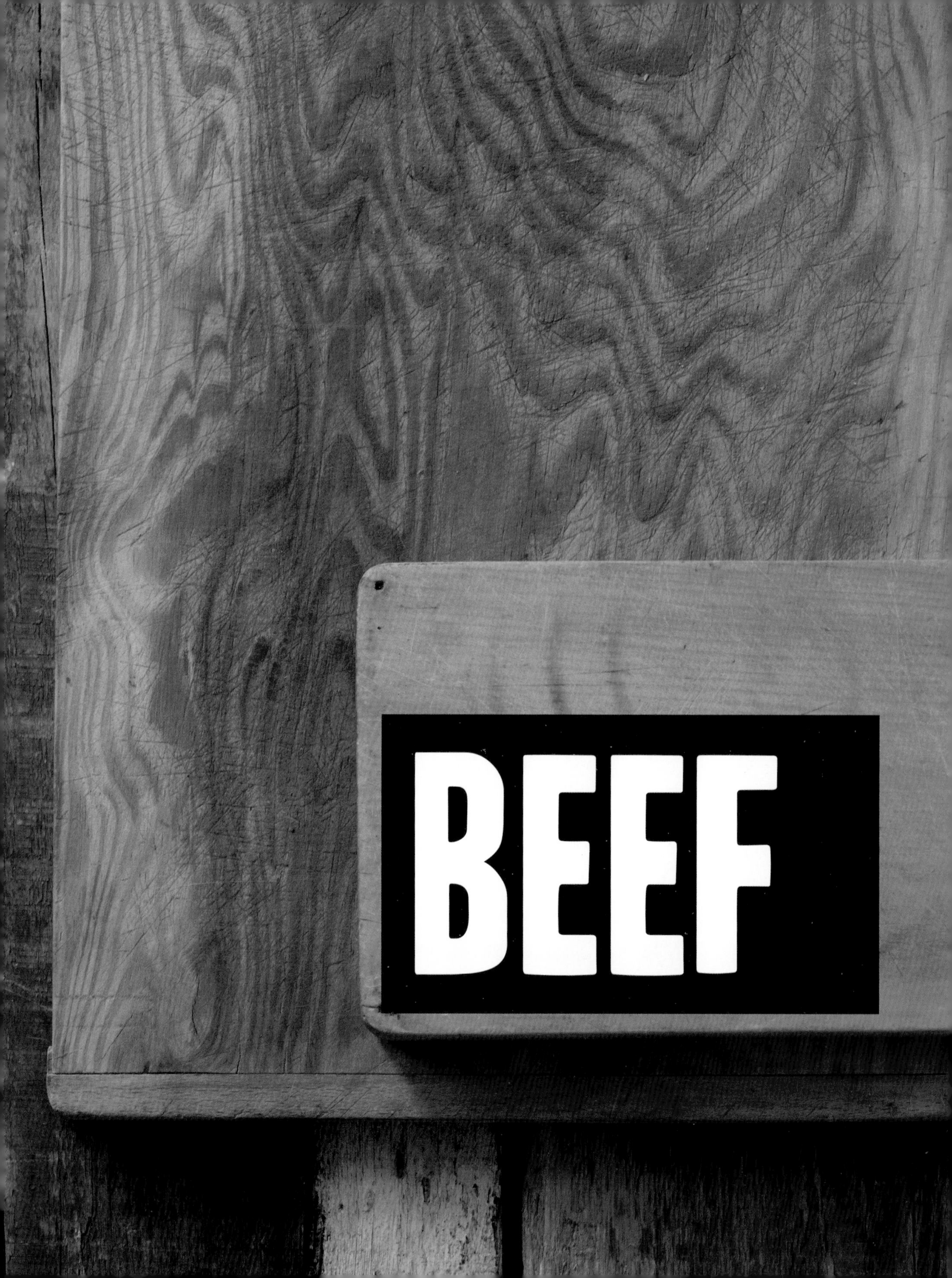
BEEF

COWS EAT GRASS, LEAVES AND VEGETABLES ALL THEIR LIVES AND CONVERT IT TO MEAT. EATING STEAK IS LIKE EATING VITAMIN PILLS.

T-BONE STEAKS WITH CHILLI BUTTER

In this recipe your steaks will be on fire, in more ways than one. First you braai them on the coals of a wood fire, and then you serve them with a fiery-spiced butter. You can prepare the butter ahead of time and theoretically it will last in your fridge for weeks (but in real life you'll probably finish it before then). It's no secret that I prefer dry-aged steaks (to their wet-aged counterparts) and a T-bone steak dry-ages well. Don't marinate the steaks, just add some salt before, during or after the braai as you see fit. Once the steaks are braaied, you put a piece of spiced butter on each, and let them rest like that for a few minutes, with the butter melting into them while your guests get ready for the feast.

WHAT YOU NEED (serves 10)

250 g butter at room temperature (soft, but not melted)

2 fresh chillies (finely chopped, or 1 tsp chilli flakes)

1 tsp cayenne pepper (or ground peri-peri)

1 tsp paprika

1 tot parsley (finely chopped)

1 tsp lemon juice

1 tsp coarse salt flakes

a grind of black pepper

1 T-bone steak per person

WHAT TO DO

1. Using electric beaters, a food processor, or a wooden spoon and some effort, beat/whisk/process all of the ingredients (except the steak of course) until mixed well.

2. If you are feeling fancy, tip the mixture onto a layer of plastic wrap or greaseproof baking paper, then shape it into a log. Twist the ends to close the log and keep it in the fridge until you're ready to use it. If you are not feeling fancy, you can just leave the soft butter in the container that you mixed it in, and use a teaspoon to dish it up later.

3. Braai the T-bone steaks for between 8 and 10 minutes on very hot coals and turn them only once. If you're wondering whether your coals are hot enough, they aren't! If you're wondering whether your steaks are cut too thin, they are! Add salt before, during or after the braai as you prefer. Although you should turn steaks on the braai once only, the shape of the T-bone steak does allow you one extra trick – if you'd like to make use of it, you can stand the steaks upright on the flat bone part for the final few minutes on the braai. That back side of the bone tends to burn black quite easily, but that's not a crisis, as you're not even going to eat the meat and spit out the bones. You're not going to eat the bone in the first place.

4. Once the steaks are braaied, put them either on a serving platter or straight onto each guest's plate. Put some spiced butter on each steak so that the butter can melt into the steak while it rests for a few minutes until you eat.

AND ...

If you like your food even hotter than this recipe, you could add more finely chopped chilli or chilli powder to the butter.

THE BRAAI GATSBY

The Gatsby sandwich is a cult classic in the Western Cape. It's traditionally served on the long white bread roll known as a baguette and is stuffed with generous helpings of your favourite ingredients. Our choice of meat for the braai Gatsby is masala-spiced steak. Commercially sold Gatsbys usually contain French fries, but we're going one up on that by including home-made potato röstis instead.

WHAT YOU NEED

(serves at least 6)

600 g rump or sirloin steak
(in total, can be two smaller pieces)

½ tot oil

½ tot masala spice

salt and freshly ground black pepper

1 large baguette

soft butter
(for spreading on the bread)

some crisp lettuce leaves
(washed)

2–3 ripe tomatoes (sliced)

2 onions (caramelised –
see page 50 for how to do this)

1 cup Cheddar cheese (grated)

½ cup mayonnaise

½ tsp peri-peri powder

all the ingredients for röstis
(see page 166)

WHAT TO DO

1. Coat the steak with oil, then season it evenly with the masala spice. It's best to do this spicing a few hours before the braai, or even the previous day. If you reckon the steak might be tough, no one will complain if you give it a few good whacks with a meat mallet before spicing it, especially not me.

2. Make the potato röstis (see page 166).

3. Braai the steak over very hot coals for 4 minutes a side, then take it off the fire. Leave it on a wooden board to rest a few minutes.

4. While the steak is taking a nap, cut the bread open lengthways (but not completely through) and spread butter on the inside. Keeping it open, toast the buttered side over the coals for a minute or two.

5. To assemble the Gatsby, put a few lettuce leaves on the bottom half of the bread. Then add slices of tomato and pack rösti pieces on top of that.

6. Slice the steak into thin strips and add to the baguette together with the caramelised onion and Cheddar cheese.

7. Mix the peri-peri into the mayo and spread it onto the inside top half of the baguette. Logic dictates that the more peri-peri you mix into the mayo, the hotter it will be, so use your common sense to adjust the burn to your liking.

8. Close the sandwich and slice into four pieces.

AND ...

In the first step of this recipe, I advise you to whack the steak a few times with a meat mallet if you think that it's going to be tough. This is general advice not only applicable to this recipe. If you think your steak is going to be tough, slap it in the face a few times until it drops that attitude. I've been to the odd well-known steakhouse that uses this method to tenderise their steaks; they just don't talk about it. Obviously, it is better to buy proper dry-aged steaks that do not need any further treatment, but for a recipe like this that is a waste of money. I just use normal wet-aged supermarket meat.

BOLOGNESE

My family started making spaghetti bolognese on the fire during camping trips in Botswana and Namibia when I was a teenager. As much as I like braaied steak and boerewors, you can't eat that every day. The secret to a great bolognese sauce is to simmer it over low coals for a few hours. The problem with cooking something that smells this good for 3 hours when camping in the Central Kalahari Game Reserve is that a pride of lions might smell it as well and pay your camp a visit, as happened to us one evening. We ate in the car that night.

WHAT YOU NEED (serves 4–6)

2 tots olive oil

1 onion (finely chopped)

1 carrot (grated)

1 celery stick (finely chopped)

500 g lean beef mince

200–250 g smoked streaky bacon (diced)

½ tot mixed dried herbs
(or 1 tot finely chopped fresh herbs like basil, thyme and parsley)

½ cup dry red wine

2 tins tomatoes (see page 10 for more on tomato tins)

2 tots tomato paste

1 tsp sugar

½ tot lemon juice

1 tsp salt

1 tsp ground black pepper

½ cup cream (optional)

To serve:

500 g pasta like tagliatelle or spaghetti

Parmesan cheese (grated or shaved)

WHAT TO DO

1. Heat oil in a potjie over a medium-hot fire. Add the onion, carrot and celery and gently fry for 5–10 minutes until the onions are soft and shiny but not brown.

2. Add the mince, bacon and herbs to the pot and fry for 10 minutes until the meat starts to brown. Stir often and break up any lumps in the mince. You want the bottom of the pot to become slightly brown and sticky here and there, as this adds flavour to the meal, but you don't want it to actually burn.

3. Pour in the wine and stir well. Use your spoon to scrape and loosen any bits of meat or other matter stuck to the bottom of the pot. Cook until the wine is almost completely reduced.

4. Now add the tomatoes, tomato paste, sugar, lemon juice, salt and pepper. Stir well and bring to a simmer over low heat. Put the lid on the pot and simmer for 2 hours, stirring every 20–30 minutes to ensure that the sauce doesn't cook dry and burn. You need very low and gentle heat, exactly the opposite of braaing steak. (If the pot runs dry, add a bit of water.)

5. After 2 hours, take off the lid and simmer uncovered for another 20-odd minutes. While you enjoy the aroma, keep a close eye on the pot – you want the sauce to reduce and thicken but not burn. During this time, cook the pasta in salted water in a separate pot.

6. When you're happy with the bolognese sauce, stir in the cream (optional) and serve the sauce with the pasta and a handful of grated Parmesan.

AND …

Pasta, like spaghetti and tagliatelle, takes about 7–8 minutes in plenty of rapidly boiling salted water to become *al dente*, which means 'just cooked with a slight bite to it'. For 500 g of pasta you need about 5 litres of water and ½ tot of salt. Don't overcook pasta or it will become a soggy mess. When it's done, drain the water off and immediately drizzle the pasta with olive oil to stop it sticking to itself.

RUMP SOSATIES WITH HOME-MADE SWEET CHILLI SAUCE

Making your own sweet chilli sauce is quite easy and takes about 10 minutes in total, so it can be done during the half-time break of a rugby game you're watching on TV. The sauce goes well with many types and cuts of meat but, like a loose forward doing his job on a rugby field, it's quite dominant. So you want to pair it with something that won't only complement but also soak up the flavour; something like real good rump sosaties that you have assembled at home. Do note that this sauce is a bit hotter than the commercial stuff sold at supermarkets. If you want it less potent, use fewer chillies.

WHAT YOU NEED (serves 4)

For the sweet chilli sauce:

5 chillies (any type or a combination, and have a few extra on standby)

2 cloves garlic
(crushed or chopped)

½ cup cider vinegar (or rice vinegar or white grape vinegar)

½ cup water

½ cup sugar

1 tsp salt

1 tsp soy sauce

½ tot cornflour mixed with ½ tot water

For the sosaties:

1 kg thick-cut rump steak

½ cup soy sauce

WHAT TO DO

Make the sauce:

1. Chop the chillies finely. If you don't want too much burn in the sauce, remove some or all of the seeds. If you like it hot, leave the seeds in. If you think the chillies you have are quite mild, use more than 5 chillies. If you think the chillies you have are particularly potent, use your common sense and good luck!

2. Mix the half tot of cornflour with a half tot of water in a suitable cup, glass or mug and keep on hand.

3. Throw the chopped chillies, garlic, vinegar, water, sugar, salt and soy sauce into a small flameproof pan or potjie, then stir well and bring to a simmer over some coals or a few flames.

4. Simmer for about 6 minutes, until the sugar has dissolved completely; the exact time will obviously depend on your coals or flames.

5. Now add the cornflour mixture from step 2 to the sauce and stir until the sauce gets thicker. This will take about 1 minute.

6. The sauce is now ready. Remove from the fire, cool slightly and serve. Alternatively pour it into a clean glass jar, close the lid and store it in the fridge until ready to use.

Make the rump sosaties:

1. Buy the thickest rump steaks you can find. The best idea is to visit a butcher and have him or her cut you some rump steaks about 3 or 4 cm thick.

2. Cut the rump steaks into blocks of about 3 cm to 4 cm square, but this is really not an exact science.

3. Throw all the cubes of meat into a marinating bowl and pour the soy sauce over it. Toss the meat until all of it is coated with the sauce. Cover the bowl and leave to marinate for at least 30 minutes before the braai.

4. Skewer the meat on four skewers.

5. Braai the sosaties for about 8–10 minutes on hot coals until just past medium rare and serve with the sweet chilli sauce.

BEEF BURGER WITH BACON AND A CHEESE SAUCE

I don't think there is any single definitive set of burger toppings but some, like cheese and bacon, are certainly more popular than others. At the time of writing this book, this is my favourite way of making beef burgers at home. The flavour of your cheese sauce depends directly on the quality and taste of the cheese you use.

WHAT YOU NEED (serves 6)

For the cheese sauce:

2 tots butter

2 tots cake flour

2 cups milk (full cream, obviously)

1 tot Dijon mustard

at least 1 cup grated mature cheese (1 cup of grated cheese is about 100 g, but err on the side of extravagance – I use a mixture of Cheddar, Parmesan and whatever else happens to be in my fridge)

salt and black pepper to taste (not all cheese has the same salt content)

For the burgers:

1 kg good-quality beef mince

1 tot olive oil

salt and pepper (optional)

1 packet smoked streaky bacon (200–250 g)

6 hamburger rolls (sliced open and buttered on the insides)

lettuce leaves (washed and drained)

2 large tomatoes (sliced)

WHAT TO DO

Make the cheese sauce:

1. Melt the butter in a pot over medium heat and then add the flour. Stir until the flour is mixed smoothly with the butter, and then cook for 1 minute, stirring all the time.

2. Pour in the milk bit by bit while stirring vigorously to incorporate it completely and make a smooth sauce. A wooden spoon should work fine, but if you struggle, use a metal hand whisk. Never leave the sauce unattended; believe me, I speak from experience. If at any time you feel you're losing control, decrease the amount of heat reaching the pot and first fully combine everything already in the pot before adding more milk.

3. As soon as all the milk has been incorporated, toss in the mustard and cheese. Stir well until the cheese has melted.

4. Take the pot off the heat and test for seasoning. Add salt and pepper if the sauce needs it. Some cheeses are very salty already and the sauce will only need a decent grinding of black pepper. Keep the sauce aside until the burgers are ready. Reheat and stir just before pouring it over the burgers – and don't worry about that 'skin' forming on top of the sauce, for it stirs away. Alternatively, make the sauce while braaing the patties.

Make the burgers:

1. Divide the mince into 6 balls, then use your clean wet hands to shape them into patties. Always flatten them a little more than you think, because they will shrink and thicken in the middle during the braai. Brush them with olive oil on both sides.

2. Put the patties on an open grid and season the top with salt and pepper. Cook for about 5 minutes, then carefully (yet confidently) flip them over with a metal spatula. Season with salt and pepper, and cook for another 5 minutes on the other side – 10 minutes in total. To be clear, you only turn the patties once on the braai. Every time you turn them, there is a risk of breaking them. Don't fiddle with the patties while they are on the braai, because it only makes you look like a beginner.

3. While you're braaing the patties, also braai the bacon until crispy. You can do this in a pan, or you can lay the rashers out on the braai grid, and also only turn them once. Take care not to drop any bacon through the grid onto the coals.

4. Put the sliced rolls buttered side down on the grid, then toast until they are golden brown. Take them off the fire. Don't burn the rolls; it happens easily.

5. To assemble the burgers: Put a piece of lettuce and 2 slices of tomato on the bottom half of the roll. The strips of crispy bacon go on next, then the braaied patty. Top it off with a generous helping of warm cheese sauce.

BEEF TRINCHADO POTJIE

Apart from being the first tourists to dock a ship at Mossel Bay, the Portuguese are also famous for a few culinary achievements. One of their best is the rich garlic and chilli-flavoured beef stew known as trinchado. Theoretically, the quantity of ingredients in this recipe means that you can serve 8 people, but in my experience it's one of those meals that are just too good, which means everyone wants second helpings.

WHAT YOU NEED (serves 6–8)

2 kg steak cubes (I use a combination of rib-eye and rump, cut into 4 cm cubes)

2 tots soy sauce

2 tots olive oil

2 tots butter

2 onions (finely chopped)

10 garlic cloves (crushed or chopped)

½ tot cayenne pepper (or chilli powder)

3 bay leaves

2 cups beef stock

½ cup brandy (no, not a printing error)

½ cup red wine (no, not a printing error)

½ tot salt

1 tsp black pepper

a big handful of pitted black olives (this is not an exact science)

1 cup cream (250 ml tub)

grated rind of a small lemon

WHAT TO DO

1. Pour the soy sauce over the steak cubes. Now you need to fry the meat to seal in the juices and you'll have to do this in batches. Generate some proper heat in your potjie by placing flames directly under it. Then add a tot of oil and a tot of butter and fry about one-third of the meat, or as much as fits in the bottom of the potjie. You could of course fry all of the meat at once if your potjie is big enough. Take the cubes out and keep to one side. Add another tot of oil and butter and fry the next third. By the time you get to the last batch of steak cubes there will be enough oil and fat left in the potjie.

2. When the last batch of meat is browned, put back all the other meat into the potjie, unless you fried it all at once. Add the onions, garlic, cayenne pepper and bay leaves; then fry for about 10 minutes until the onions are soft.

3. Pour in the beef stock, brandy, wine, salt and pepper. Heat until the sauce starts to simmer, then cover with a lid and continue to gently simmer for 1 hour until the meat is very tender.

4. Remove the lid and stir in the olives, cream and lemon rind. Bring to the boil and then cook for a further 10 minutes, uncovered, until the sauce starts to get thicker.

5. Remove from the fire and let it stand for a few minutes before serving. The generous amount of sauce is part of this meal and should be enjoyed with the meat, so serve trinchado in bowls and eat the sauce with spoons when necessary.

AND …

I know it sounds like a bit of a mission to grate lemon rind, but in some instances you really have to do it, this being one of those cases. Grating the rind of a lemon is really not a challenging job; it smells nice and it'll make you look like the type of expert who reads this book. It adds a unique flavour to this dish that would just not be the same without it.

FILLET WITH RED WINE SAUCE

It's a well-recognised fact that braaied steak goes well with red wine. What is further undisputed is that a steak braaied over the coals of an open wood fire has a unique, rather good taste. What we're doing here is combining these universally accepted truths to create something that is, dare I say it, beautiful!

WHAT YOU NEED (serves 4)

1 kg fillet steak
(or slightly bigger)

1 tot butter

½ onion
(chopped as finely as you can)

1 clove garlic
(chopped very finely)

1 tsp fresh thyme leaves

½ tot flour

1½ cups red wine

½ cup beef stock

1½ tots sugar

1 tsp balsamic vinegar

salt and freshly ground black pepper

WHAT TO DO

1. Light a relatively big fire using your favourite braai wood.

2. Remove the steak from its packaging. Rinse it under cold running water and pat dry with kitchen towels. Cut it into four equally sized portions and then season them well with salt and pepper. Don't be shy with the pepper. Cover the steak to keep it safe from flies and proceed to the next step.

3. Place a medium-sized flameproof pan or potjie over the fire. You want a pretty high heat but it must not be searing hot, so just use some of the burning logs under the potjie, not all of them.

4. Melt the butter and then fry the onions, garlic and thyme leaves for about 5 minutes until the onion is soft and starts to turn brown. If you're a regular user of this book and are tuned in to the finer things in life, fry the onions first and add the garlic about 1 minute before the next step.

5. Add the flour and stir well, then immediately add the red wine, stock, sugar and vinegar. Mix well, bring to the boil and then boil over high heat to reduce the liquid by half. Stir often. Depending on the size of your pot and the heat of your fire, this should take 15 minutes, but it could be slightly longer or slightly shorter. While the liquid is reducing, it should thicken and become a rich sauce. Taste the sauce at this point and season with salt and pepper. Keep in mind that some beef stocks are already quite salty, so you might not need salt at all. When you're happy with the texture of the sauce, remove from the fire.

6. While you're waiting for the sauce to reduce in step 5, braai the steaks over very high heat for about 8–10 minutes. Braai them on all four or six sides. That's right, when you slice a 1 kg fillet steak into 4 pieces the shape of the fillet steaks can have four or six sides.

7. Serve the steaks on warm plates and pour the red wine sauce over them.

AND ...

The truth of the matter is that you could serve this sauce with any other cut of beautifully braaied steak. Personally, I'm quite attached to serving it with fillet because although fillet is so wonderfully tender, the sauce gives it that little kick of extra flavour it needs.

BRAISED OXTAIL

In the culinary world, a good oxtail stew is one of the global supermodels. Oxtail is a very tough cut of meat full of the connective tissue collagen, and you can't just braai it on a grid. The only way to prepare oxtail is to cook it for a really long time at a relatively low temperature. What happens then is that the collagen dissolves into gelatine, which gives a typical oxtail dish its rich, full flavour. This recipe is not particularly difficult, but it does take time and needs patience, so start the process well ahead of serving time. As a guide, if your meal's kick-off time is 8pm, get going at about 3pm.

WHAT YOU NEED (serves 6)

2 kg oxtail pieces

1 tot olive oil

1 onion (chopped or rings)

3 cloves garlic
(chopped or crushed)

1 tsp chilli powder

1 cup port wine (use red wine if you don't have port)

1 cup water

potentially some extra liquid
(port, water, beef stock)

1 tsp salt

1 tsp ground black pepper

250 g button mushrooms

1 cup cream (250 ml tub)

2 tots peach chutney

WHAT TO DO

1. Choose a potjie from your arsenal that is big enough for you to be able to put all the browned oxtail pieces in a single layer, more or less, on the bottom of the potjie. Fry the oxtail pieces in oil in the potjie for about 10 minutes until well and truly browned.

2. Add the onion, garlic and chilli powder and fry for another few minutes until the onion goes a bit brown.

3. Now add the port, water, salt and pepper. Close the lid and set your cruise control to a gentle simmer; you want to go low and slow from here on. Adjust the heat by taking away some coals so that the liquid is only just simmering. Basically, the meat will simmer like that for 5 hours in total. Check in every hour or so to see that the temperature is steady and add coals under the potjie as and when necessary. Add a little bit of extra port, water or beef stock if at any stage of the process there is too much heat and the liquid is reducing too quickly. After about 2 or 3 hours, turn each oxtail piece over so that the part that was facing down now faces upwards, and vice versa.

4. With 90 minutes to go (after about 3½ hours), lift the lid, quickly throw in the mushrooms, cream and peach chutney, and close the lid again.

5. The meat must be very soft and should easily come off the bones when you eat it, but it shouldn't cook off the bone in the potjie – this is not a soup. After about 4½ hours in total, take off the lid and test to see if the oxtail is starting to come loose from the bone. If not, close the lid and continue cooking until it does.

6. When the oxtail is really tender, taste the meal and season with salt and pepper, then stir carefully.

7. Serve with parsley-flavoured mashed potato.

HOW TO MAKE PARSLEY-FLAVOURED MASHED POTATO

1. Wash 6 medium-to-large potatoes, then boil them in salted water until very soft. When their skins start to burst, you'll know they are ready.

2. You don't need to peel the potatoes. Discard all the water from the pot and use a masher to mash the potatoes. Remove and discard all large pieces of potato skin that get stuck on the masher, but leave the other bits of skin in the mash; it adds to the flavour.

3. Stir in 2 tots of butter or cream and 2 tots of chopped, fresh parsley. Add salt and pepper to taste.

STEAK AND STOUT PIE

The Irish have their own version of National Braai Day, called St Patrick's Day – the day their country comes to a standstill and has one big party. I've been to some St Patrick's Day celebrations in Dublin as part of my ongoing research and development of National Braai Day. Every single pub in Ireland serves a fantastic pie made with steak and stout. I've adapted their recipe to suit our local braai conditions. You make the pie filling in a potjie and you braai the pastry on a grid over the coals. Easy as pie!

WHAT YOU NEED (serves 6)

2 tots olive oil

1 kg steak (chuck is best, otherwise rump; cut into blocks of 2 cm × 2 cm)

2 tsp salt

1 tsp black pepper

1 tot cake flour

1 onion (finely chopped)

1 carrot (peeled and finely chopped)

2 sticks celery (finely chopped)

1 tot chopped mixed herbs (rosemary, thyme, parsley; or use ½ tot dried mixed herbs)

1 can or bottle stout (about 400 ml)

250 g button mushrooms (halved)

1 packet puff pastry (400 g, completely thawed)

WHAT TO DO

1. Heat the olive oil in a large flat-bottomed potjie over a hot fire. Add the steak cubes, salt and pepper and stir. Shake in the flour, and then stir well to distribute the flour evenly over everything. The bottom of the pot will seem a bit dry, but don't worry too much about it. Fry for about 5 minutes until the pieces of flour-coated meat turn golden brown.

2. Add the onion, carrot, celery and herbs, then fry for another 5 minutes.

3. Now pour in the stout. Stir to loosen any sticky bits on the bottom of the pot, and then bring to a simmer. Cover and simmer gently for 15 minutes.

4. Add the mushrooms, cover the pot, and then simmer over low heat for 1 hour. It is very important to keep the heat low. 'Low heat' means a few coals, and no flames of any significance under the pot.

5. When the pie filling in the potjie is nearly ready (after about 1 hour of total cooking time), unroll the puff pastry from the packet. Now you have two options: either cut the pastry into the shape of the bowls you're going to serve the pies in, or cut it into squares that you will put on top of the filling on plates or in bowls. Braai the pastry shapes in an oiled, closed hinged grid for about 20 minutes over very mild coals. Turn the grid often until the pastry is golden brown and crispy. Don't braai them too fast, as there is a good chance they will burn if you do. The pastry will look like it is starting to 'melt' at first; don't worry, it will soon firm up and become easier to handle if you just carefully turn it quite often.

6. When the filling is ready, take the potjie off the fire and stir well. The liquid should be thick and glossy. If not, cook uncovered for a few minutes to let it reduce and thicken. Taste and add salt and pepper if necessary.

7. Serve by dishing up the filling into bowls or onto plates and then put the braaied pieces of pastry on top of each of them. You could also serve the pies with mashed potatoes if you like.

AND …

Although Guinness is the internationally famous example of stout, it's by no means the only one. You can make this recipe just as effectively with a local favourite like Castle Milk Stout.

SHISH KEBABS

Shish kebabs are a Turkish version of what we generally call sosaties. The Turks love to skewer spicy marinated meat with tomatoes, peppers, onions and mushrooms, and I reckon they're on the money. Let the meat marinate overnight to allow the flavours to develop to their full potential, and for the meat to absorb them properly.

WHAT YOU NEED

(makes 6–8 kebabs)

For the marinade:

½ cup olive oil

½ cup lemon juice

½ tot ground cumin

½ tot ground paprika

½ tot ground coriander

½ tot dried oregano

1 tsp salt

½ tsp black pepper

For the kebabs:

1 kg steak (rump, sirloin, rib-eye or fillet, cut into 3 cm × 3 cm cubes)

2 onions (cut into large chunks, with layers separated)

2 peppers (green, yellow or red – seeds and stalks removed, and cut into square chunks)

250 g small button mushrooms (whole)

250 g cherry tomatoes

WHAT TO DO

1. Throw all the ingredients for the marinade together in a marinating bowl and mix well. Toss the beef cubes into the mix and stir until all the pieces are coated in marinade. Cover the bowl and marinate for at least 3 hours (on your counter or somewhere in the shade), but preferably overnight. Whenever you feel like it, you can visit the meat and stir it around before putting it back in the fridge.

2. Around the time that you're lighting the fire for your braai, remove the marinated meat from the fridge and wash your hands for the assembling process. Skewer the beef cubes by alternating with pieces of onion, peppers, whole mushrooms and cherry tomatoes, packing them tightly together. Brush the assembled kebabs with any leftover marinade.

3. Braai the kebabs for about 8 minutes over hot coals. The kebabs can be quite fragile, so braaing them in a hinged grid that you close gently is the way to go.

AND …

If you're in the middle of the Karoo and find yourself with an ample supply of good yet affordable lamb, use chunks of that for your shish kebabs instead of beef.

BRAAIED MASALA BEEF MARROW BONES

Eating braaied marrow bones is quite decadent. Enjoy them spread on warm fire-toasted bread with a glass of ice-cold white wine. Ask your butcher (at the butchery or behind the supermarket meat counter) for thick-cut beef marrow bones that you want to braai. They should have some available or will be able to cut them right there for you. Shin bones work well. You'll find the wider the bones, the easier it will be to get the marrow out after the braai.

WHAT YOU NEED

(serves 6 as a starter)

1½–2 kg beef marrow bones (cut into 5 cm-thick pieces)

1 tot olive oil

2 tots garam masala

salt and black pepper

bread (to serve)

lemon wedges (to serve)

WHAT TO DO

1. Brush the marrow bones with oil, dust with the garam masala, and season with salt and pepper.

2. Lie all the bones flat on a hinged grid, open sides facing up and down, and close the grid. If your marrow bones are too thick to fit inside a hinged grid, just braai them on an open grid and turn them regularly with braai tongs.

3. Braai the bones for about 20–25 minutes over hot coals, turning occasionally. The exact time will naturally depend on the heat of your fire. You'll see that the marrow starts to swell at the ends of the bones when it's almost ready. Test one marrow bone by taking it off the fire and scooping out the marrow. If the marrow is still slightly pink or red, braai the bones for a further 5–10 minutes. Don't be alarmed if the outside of the bones turns very dark and toasty; this is exactly what we're looking for in order for the marrow inside to be fully cooked.

4. When you're almost finished braaing the marrow bones, toast a few slices of bread on the side of the grid until golden brown.

5. When the marrow bones are ready, take them off the fire and serve with the freshly toasted bread, fresh lemon wedges and salt flakes. The marrow should come out of the bones easily when asked to do so by a normal knife.

AND …

Garam masala is available at any spice shop worth its braai salt.

CHILLI CON CARNE

Chilli con carne works equally well for breakfast, brunch, lunch or dinner. Perfect for a surf trip, hunting trip or anywhere else you might want to serve a warm and spicy meal to a hungry crowd! The nice thing is that it actually improves after standing a few hours, so you could prepare it in your potjie, and then go into the sea or veld, and upon your return when everyone is cold and hungry, you can just warm it up and bask in the glory.

Don't be put off by the fairly long list of ingredients – the method makes up for it as it's very straightforward. Serve it as is or with a piece of bread.

WHAT YOU NEED (serves 4)

2 tots olive oil

2 onions (finely chopped)

4 cloves garlic (crushed or chopped)

1 red pepper (seeds and stalks removed, then chopped)

500 g lean beef mince

1 carrot (grated)

1 tsp paprika

1 tsp ground cumin

1 tsp chilli powder (or cayenne pepper)

1 tsp ground coriander

2 cans chopped tomatoes

1 tot tomato paste (or 1 × 50 g sachet)

1 can borlotti beans (drained and rinsed under cold water)

1 can chickpeas (drained and rinsed under cold water)

1 tot vinegar

½ tot sugar

½ tot salt

1 tsp black pepper

1 cup sour cream (250 ml tub, to serve)

fresh coriander leaves (to serve)

WHAT TO DO

1. Heat the oil in a potjie over a hot fire. Add the onions, garlic and red pepper and fry for 5–10 minutes until the onions are soft and the edges start to turn a bit brown.

2. Tip in the mince, stir and break up any lumps with a wooden spoon. Fry for about 10 minutes until the beef starts to 'catch' on the bottom of the pan, taking care not to let it burn.

3. Add the carrot, paprika, cumin, chilli powder and coriander, and stir well.

4. To this, throw in the tomatoes, tomato paste, beans, chickpeas, vinegar, sugar, salt and pepper, and then stir well.

5. Bring the mixture to the boil, then cook for about 15 minutes, stirring every now and then to make sure it doesn't burn on the bottom.

6. Remove from the fire and serve with a dollop (ja, I know, I don't like the word 'dollop' either, but the editor insisted that it's the best way to describe it; so there you go, 'dollop' made it into the final draft of my book) of sour cream and some fresh coriander leaves. Alternatively, you could take the potjie off the fire, let it rest somewhere with the lid on, and reheat it a few hours later before serving.

AND …

If you're planning to prepare this meal when you're on the road, don't pack all the bottles and packs of spices. Just measure them out at home and throw them together in one small bag or container.

STEAK WITH MUSTARD AND BRANDY BUTTER

The flavour of mustard, butter and brandy is a perfect match for a braaied steak. These days most classy people know that steak should be enjoyed medium rare, so that is how you should braai it. Make the flavoured butter before your braai and keep it in the fridge until you need it.

WHAT YOU NEED (serves 10)

250 g salted butter at room temperature (very soft, but not melted)

2 tots mustard (preferably whole-grain, otherwise Dijon or English)

2 tots brandy

1 tot parsley (finely chopped)

1 tsp lemon juice

1 tsp black pepper

steaks (1 per person)

WHAT TO DO

1. Mix all the ingredients really well in a bowl, except the steak of course.

2. Put the flavoured butter mixture into a nice-looking bowl that you can serve it from. Cover the bowl with cling wrap or foil and refrigerate until ready to use. You can do these first two steps hours or even days in advance.

3. Take the butter out of the fridge just before you light your fire to braai the steaks. This way it won't be rock hard when you serve it.

4. Braai the steaks for 4 minutes on each side over very hot coals until medium rare. For a comprehensive description of exactly how I think steak should be braaied, see pages 9–10 of my first book, *Fireworks*.

5. First plate the braaied steaks and then put a good blob of butter on top of each steak. As the butter melts on the meat, the brandy and mustard flavour seeps into it.

AND ...

Of course you can experiment with the above list of ingredients and develop your own personal style of flavoured butter to serve with braaied steak.

In step 2 you can also make a log of butter by wrapping the mixture in cling wrap or wax paper before putting it in the fridge instead of storing it in a bowl. Then, in step 4, you can slice it and put discs of butter on each steak.

BEEF MADRAS CURRY

One of the best things about Britain is not British at all; it's Indian. The Brits love their Indian curries and the Madras curry, named after the South Indian town with the same name (now called Chennai) is right up there. The dish has some distinctive flavour notes (as those wine-tasting people would say), which you'll pick up if you make it with all the correct ingredients as listed below. Madras curry is traditionally very hot, so if the thought of a chilli makes you sweat, rather move along to some other page, or stay here for a delicious meal but leave out the chilli powder. The spices listed below are all things that should be standard items in your kitchen, so if you need to buy some don't worry, they won't go to waste – you'll use them for many other recipes in this book.

WHAT YOU NEED (serves 4–6)

2 tots vegetable oil

1 onion (finely chopped)

1 tsp cinnamon

2 cardamom pods

½ tot cumin seeds
(or aniseed – but not star anise)

½ tot ground coriander

½ tot chilli powder (optional)

½ tot paprika

1 tsp turmeric

½ tot garam masala

1 kg beef
(boneless, cut into chunks)

½ tot salt

1 tsp black pepper

4 cloves garlic (finely chopped)

1 tot crushed fresh ginger
(or grated)

1 can chopped tomatoes

1 can coconut milk

juice of 1 lemon

**1 punnet fresh coriander
leaves**

WHAT TO DO

1. Heat the oil in a potjie over a medium-sized fire. Add the onion and fry for a few minutes until it's soft but not brown.

2. Now the spices go in: cinnamon, cardamom, cumin, coriander, chilli powder (optional), paprika, turmeric and garam masala. Stir for a minute until it starts smelling irresistible. Right about now what I call the 'word of nose' phenomenon will kick in. Your neighbours will start calling to invite themselves over for dinner. Stay focused and look at the bottom of the potjie, which might seem very dry. Proceed immediately to the next step.

3. Add the beef, salt, pepper, garlic and ginger. Fry for a few minutes until the meat starts to brown on all sides. The beef will release some juices. Use this to scrape away any sticky bits of spices at the bottom of the potjie. If you struggle, add a very small amount of water to help you.

4. Pour in the tomatoes, coconut milk and lemon juice. Bring to a very slight simmer, then cover and cook over a few coals (no flames) for 90 minutes until the meat is tender. Don't confuse tender meat with a government tender. Tender meat is a good thing.

5. Serve on rice (see page 182) with a yoghurt and cucumber sauce called raita (see page 86) and fresh coriander leaves.

AND …

If your potjie is fairly small and the meat will not be able to brown properly all at the same time, do that in batches first, before you brown the onions. Then set the browned meat aside and simply add it back to the potjie in step 3.

STEAK BURGER WITH CORIANDER AND PERI-PERI SAUCE

This sauce is a real crowd pleaser and you can enjoy it with lots of braaied meats, especially steak and chicken. Prepare the sauce before your braai so you can act all casual when your guests are there. Only turn the steaks once when you're braaing them, keeping up your cool appearance. No one will suspect a thing until their first bite.

WHAT YOU NEED

For the sauce (makes enough sauce for about 8–10 burgers):

½ **cup mayonnaise**

½ **cup chutney**

5 cloves garlic (crushed or grated)

3 or 4 African bird's eye chillies (stalks taken off and finely chopped)

1 tsp peri-peri powder

1 punnet (about 30 g) **fresh coriander** (finely chopped)

For the steak burger (per burger):

200 g rump steak (or sirloin steak or chicken fillet)

hamburger roll

lettuce leaf

slices of tomato

WHAT TO DO

Make the sauce:

1. Mix all the ingredients together, then use immediately or store in the fridge in an airtight container.

Make the burgers:

1. Use one 200 g rump or sirloin steak for each person. Give it a few whacks with a meat mallet to make it the same thickness all round and so that it will fit the roll comfortably. This also means that it will be easier for your teeth to bite through the meat once in the burger. In the industry we call this 'tender bite'.

2. Braai the steaks for 6–8 minutes over very hot coals until just past medium rare.

3. Put the steaks in buttered hamburger rolls together with lettuce and tomato. Top with a generous helping of the sauce and stand back to bask in the glory.

BEEF BRISKET IN A MAN-OVEN

On the American barbecue circuit, brisket is the actual test of whether a man knows his stuff. Texas is at the heart of this matter and the seasoning I use here is a sweet and spicy Texas-style rub. It's perfect for beef brisket but also works just as well on pork. The trick is to cook the meat for several hours in a man-oven using low and slow indirect heat, giving it time to become really tender. When cooked properly, the meat will taste smoky and surprisingly sweet.

WHAT YOU NEED
(serves about 6–8 people)

2.5 kg piece beef brisket
(preferably with a nice layer of fat – ask your butcher for this flat rectangular piece of meat, as he'll know just what you're looking for)

1 tot brown sugar

1 tot salt flakes
(or medium-coarse salt)

1 tot coarsely ground black pepper

1 tot paprika (or smoked paprika)

1 tot oregano

½ tot ground chilli powder
(or ground peri-peri – optional)

WHAT TO DO

1. Make the rub by mixing all the ingredients (except the meat of course) together in a small bowl.

2. Wash the meat under cold running water and pat the meat dry with a kitchen towel. Now sprinkle the rub all over the meat to generously cover the full surface of the meat and work it in with your clean hands (not all of it will stick to the meat, but try to get as much on it as possible). You can proceed to the next step immediately, or cover the meat and leave it in a fridge to absorb some flavour from the spices for a few hours.

3. Set up your man-oven for indirect grilling and bring its temperature to 110–120 °C.

4. Put the piece of meat in a foil drip tray and position the tray in the middle of the top grid of your man-oven. Close the lid then cook the brisket for at least 6 hours, regulating the temperature with the air vents to keep it between 110 and 120 °C.

5. The meat is ready when the internal temperature goes past 80 °C, which you will measure with your meat thermometer. Start checking it after about 5 hours to see how you're doing, but don't open the lid too often, because heat escapes and that slows down the process.

6. When the meat is done, take it out of the man-oven and put it on a large wooden cutting board. Cover loosely with foil, and then let it rest for 10 minutes before cutting it in thin slices (against the grain). Serve the meat as is or on sandwiches or toasted buns with things like cheese, tomato, lettuce, mayo and mustard. Another popular option is to ask your prettier half to make a gravy sauce with the drippings left in the drip pan, and to enjoy the brisket with that.

AND ...

While it is theoretically possible to do, I don't advise preparing brisket in a normal kettle braai. Your weapon of choice is a ceramic Kamado-style man-oven like my Monolith (www.monolithbraai.co.za). You load it with a bit of charcoal, light it up, regulate the temperature with the air vents, and 6 hours later you're eating like a king!

MEATBALLS IN TOMATO SAUCE

For quite a few years after university I went through a phase – let's call it 'the dark ages' – during which I did not eat meatballs. That was until my friend Martin, a big man with a big appetite, showed me one evening how great decent meatballs can taste. And so I set about developing a meatballs recipe for the braai – glory days! Your weapon of choice here is a cast-iron pan called a 'skillet', but any other flat-bottomed cast-iron pot or fireproof pan will also do the trick. The recipe works equally well with lean beef mince or ostrich mince.

WHAT YOU NEED

(serves 4, or 1 Martin)

For the meatballs:

500 g lean mince

1 cup white bread crumbs (buy at the supermarket or make your own by processing 2 slices of bread in a food processor)

1 small bunch spring onions (finely sliced)

1 tot fresh basil (finely chopped)

1 tot fresh parsley (finely chopped)

1 tsp salt

½ tsp black pepper

½ tsp dried oregano

1 egg

olive oil (for frying)

For the tomato sauce:

4 cloves garlic (crushed or chopped)

2 tots red wine

2 tins tomatoes (whole, chopped or cherry)

2 tots tomato paste

½ tot sugar

1 tsp paprika

1 tsp salt

½ tsp black pepper

To serve:

extra chopped basil or parsley

Parmesan cheese

500 g pasta (see page 20 for preparation advice)

WHAT TO DO

1. Mix together all the ingredients for the meatballs (except the olive oil) in a large bowl with your recently washed hands. Now roll balls into roughly the size of golf balls. Your aim is to have 12 meatballs. If you have one handy, use an ice-cream scoop to create meatball portions of the same size before rolling them.

2. Heat your pot or pan over medium-hot coals. Add olive oil and then fry the meatballs all at once. You need a pot or pan where all the meatballs fit into the bottom of the pot or pan in a single layer. Use tongs or a spatula to gently turn them once or twice, taking care not to break them.

3. When the meatballs are browned (but not cooked through), start making the tomato sauce by scattering the garlic into the pan with the meatballs and frying for another minute.

4. Add the wine and shake the pan lightly to loosen any brown bits on the bottom. Use a spatula to scrape off the stubborn bits that remain stuck.

5. When the wine is almost completely reduced, add the tomatoes, tomato paste, sugar, paprika, salt and pepper. Bring to the boil and then simmer uncovered over medium to low heat for about 15–20 minutes until the meatballs are cooked.

6. Take off the fire and then top with extra chopped basil and/or parsley as well as some grated or shaved Parmesan cheese. Serve immediately on a bed of pasta.

AND ...

You can prepare the meatballs hours in advance. Cover them and store in a fridge, then you can continue from step 2 when your guests arrive.

STEAK SANDWICH WITH MUSTARD, MAYO AND CARAMELISED ONIONS

People who know me know that I don't believe the only way to serve steak is in one massive and intimidating piece on a plate. Braaing a great steak can also be seen as the first step to creating something like an awesome steak sandwich. Caramelised onions are the other special part of this sandwich. Although made from the same core ingredient and similar in appearance, do not confuse caramelised onions with fried onions. The former are much sweeter owing to the longer cooking time, which gives the sugars in the onion more time to caramelise, and the flavour more time to develop. It's a good idea to make the caramelised onions ahead of your braai, leaving you time to focus on braaing the steak to perfection.

WHAT YOU NEED (serves 6)

For the caramelised onions:

4 onions (finely sliced into rings or long strips, not diced)

2 tots olive oil

3 tots brown sugar

2 tots balsamic vinegar

salt and black pepper
(for seasoning; the flavours are already quite intense, so not a lot)

For the sandwich:

1.2 kg rump or sirloin steak
(steak is usually not sold in exact weights, so buy enough steak so that you have a total weight of around 1.2 kg)

salt and pepper (for seasoning)

12 slices of bread
(fresh, good quality bread of your choice, or 6 quality rolls)

butter (for spreading on the bread rolls)

1–2 tots Dijon mustard

fresh lettuce leaves (washed)

4–6 tots mayonnaise

Make the caramelised onions:

1. In a pot or pan over medium heat (not too hot), heat the oil and add the sliced onions. Fry gently until they become soft, then continue to fry gently until they begin to turn brown and slightly caramelised from their natural sugars. This should take about 20 minutes – be patient!

2. Now add the brown sugar and vinegar and keep stirring. Cook for another 5–10 minutes, stirring often, until the liquid becomes reduced and syrupy. Season lightly with salt and pepper, stir well and remove from the heat. Cover and store the onions where flies can't attack them. You can cook the onions in advance before your guests arrive. Caramelised onions keep well in the fridge for a few days.

Assemble the sandwich:

1. Braai the steaks over very hot coals for 7–8 minutes in total until they are medium rare. You want the meat properly seasoned with salt and pepper. You can do this seasoning before, during or after the braai, depending on when you believe it's best to season meat. As you might guess, I don't think it matters when you salt the steak, because it won't make any noticeable difference to the end result of this meal.

2. The steaks need to rest before you slice them. This should be for at least 5 minutes, but can be for a few hours as well, as it's entirely acceptable to use cold steak for this sandwich. When you slice the steaks, lie them flat on a cutting board and go in at a 45-degree angle instead of straight down. This allows you to slice through the fibres in the meat an additional time, resulting in even more tender slices of meat. If you struggle to produce nice thin neat slices, you need to sharpen your chef's or carving knife, or you need a new knife altogether.

3. Butter the slices of bread. Now put them with buttered sides facing down on the grid and toast until golden brown. You do this after braaing the steaks, and while the steaks are resting. The coals might still be pretty hot, so be careful not to burn the bread. You might consider lifting the grid a bit higher.

4. Assemble the sandwich as follows: Spread each toasted bottom slice of bread with mustard and cover with some lettuce. Distribute the steak strips evenly and top with the caramelised onion. Spread the inside top half of each sandwich with mayonnaise and close. As with all recipes in this book, there is a handy full-page photo right next to this recipe to guide you in the general direction.

BEEF GOULASH

Beef goulash is Hungary's national dish – a country with a name that sounds very similar to the feeling I experience whenever I think of goulash. The signature flavour of the meal is paprika, so make sure you add it. You traditionally serve goulash on pasta and finish it off with a bit of sour cream. It's a rich warm meal that is perfect to prepare in a potjie, perhaps in winter, in a mountain hut, in front of a fireplace, while drinking red wine, for example.

WHAT YOU NEED (serves 6)

1 tot olive oil

2 onions (finely chopped)

2 cloves garlic (finely chopped)

1.5 kg boneless beef shin cubes (butcheries and supermarkets often sell 'goulash meat' or boneless stewing beef, and both are perfect for the job)

2 tots paprika

1 tsp chilli powder (optional)

1 large potato (diced into small cubes)

2 peppers (green, yellow or red; chopped)

2 tomatoes (chopped)

1 tot tomato paste

1 cup beef stock

1 tsp salt

1 tsp black pepper

500 g pasta (for serving; cooked according to instructions on the packet or as explained on page 20)

sour cream (for serving; a 250 ml tub is more than enough)

WHAT TO DO

1. Heat the oil in a potjie and fry the onions for about 4 minutes until they start to soften, then throw in the garlic. Onions take longer to cook than garlic, so always fry onions before adding the garlic. This is general advice and is not only applicable to this recipe.

2. Add the beef cubes, paprika and optional chilli powder. Fry until the beef starts to brown. If you add the chilli powder, the meal will have a bit of a kick; if you don't add it, it will have less of a kick. If you want a mild kick, just add a pinch. Your choice.

3. Add the potato cubes, peppers, tomatoes, tomato paste and beef stock, and mix to combine them all. Bring to the boil and simmer over low coals with the lid on for about 2 hours. Check every 30 minutes to stir the potjie and make sure the meat doesn't cook dry – the temperature should be just high enough to maintain a gentle simmer. You want the sauce to thicken but you don't want the meal to burn. Theoretically, you would be able to serve the meal as soon as the potatoes are soft enough to eat. The long, slow cooking is simply to enrich the flavour.

4. After 2 hours, take off the lid and season with salt and pepper to taste. Remember that you can always add more salt later, but you can never remove salt once it's in, so go easy.

5. Take the potjie off the fire and let it stand for a few minutes. Serve with freshly cooked pasta noodles and a blob of sour cream on top of the goulash.

AND …

If you have something fresh like parsley growing in the garden, garnish with that.

BOBOTIE

Bobotie is a South African classic and an important part of our culinary heritage. It's also one of my favourite meals, but this doesn't make me special: everybody loves *bobotie*. As with many other South African cult hits, you can cook it very successfully on a braai fire. I believe it's your moral duty to perfect the art of making *bobotie*. It's a great way to show off when you cook for visitors to South Africa.

WHAT YOU NEED (serves 6)

1 tot oil

3 onions (finely chopped)

3 cloves garlic (finely chopped)

2 tots medium strength curry powder

½ tot ground turmeric

1 kg beef mince

½ tot salt

1 tsp black pepper

1 cup apricot jam

½ cup raisins

½ cup almond flakes

1 tot vinegar (or lemon juice)

5 bay leaves

3 eggs

1 cup milk

rice (to serve)

chutney (to serve)

WHAT TO DO

1. Heat the oil in a flat-bottomed potjie over a medium-hot fire and fry the onions and garlic until the onions are soft but not brown.

2. Add the curry powder and turmeric, then fry for a minute – the bottom of the potjie will look quite dry, but don't let the mixture burn.

3. Chuck in the mince and fry for about 10 minutes, stirring it to break up any lumps with a wooden spoon. The mince should change colour from red to light brown, but shouldn't turn dark yet. The meat should release some juices – use these juices and your wooden spoon to loosen any sticky bits on the bottom of the potjie.

4. Add the salt and pepper, apricot jam, raisins, almond flakes and vinegar/lemon juice. Stir well, bring to a slow simmer and put on the lid. Simmer for about 15 minutes, stirring once in a while to make sure the mixture doesn't burn.

5. Now remove the lid and flatten the mixture with the back of your spoon so that it's even across the bottom of the potjie. Whisk the eggs and milk together in a small mixing bowl, then pour over the *bobotie*. Stick the bay leaves into the egg mixture. Cover with the lid and put a layer of hot coals on top of the lid. At this stage you only want coals on the lid, not underneath the potjie. Cook for 30 minutes and the *bobotie* should be ready.

6. Serve with rice (see page 182) and chutney on the side.

AND ...

Some people also like sliced banana, coconut or chopped tomatoes with their *bobotie*. Serve whichever sambals you prefer.

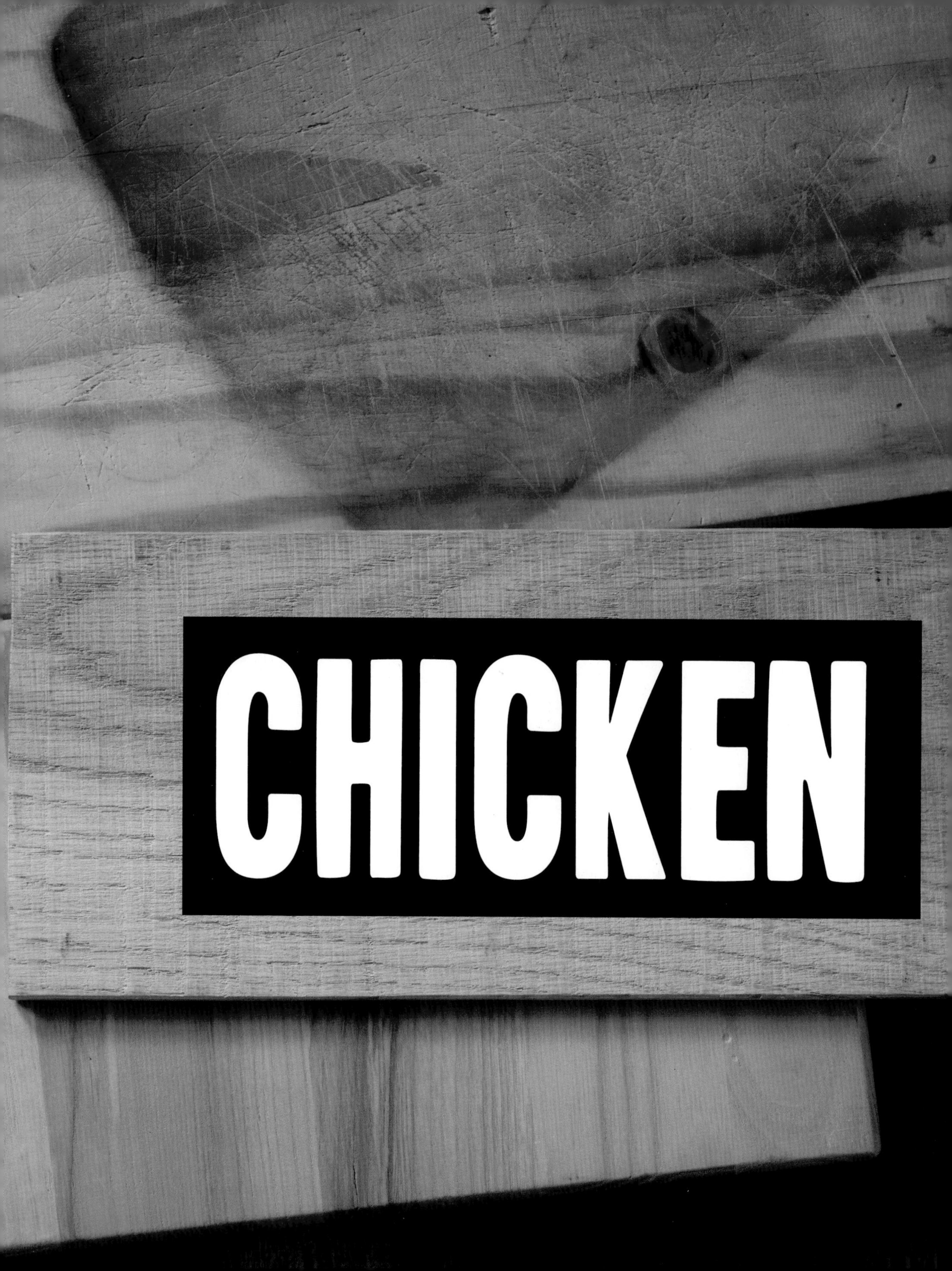
CHICKEN

COMPARED TO A WHOLE LAMB, COW OR PIG, BRAAING A WHOLE CHICKEN IS VERY STRAIGHTFORWARD. LOGICALLY THEN, BRAAING ANY PARTS OF THE WHOLE SHOULD NOT BE INTIMIDATING AT ALL.

POT ROAST CHICKEN

For this version of braaied chicken you're going the decadent extra mile. You're not just braaing it on a grid or baking it in your man-oven, you're roasting it in your potjie. We're talking whole chicken cooked in a potjie with loads of garlic and white wine, cream and herbs. When you're done you might feel the urge to do a little victory dance, but don't. Those are for rugby players when they score tries, and they're usually embarrassed about it a few years later.

WHAT YOU NEED (serves 4)

1 tot olive oil

1 onion (finely chopped)

1 packet smoked streaky bacon (about 200–250 g, finely chopped)

half a bulb of garlic (skin the cloves but leave them whole)

1 carrot (peeled and finely chopped)

1 celery stick (finely chopped)

3 sprigs fresh thyme

1 medium-sized whole chicken

1 tot brandy

1 cup dry white wine

1 tsp salt

½ tsp black pepper

½ cup cream (125 ml)

mashed potatoes or cooked white rice (to serve)

1 tot fresh parsley (chopped, for garnish)

WHAT TO DO

1. Heat the oil in your potjie (a classic shape no. 3 is perfect) over a hot fire, then add onions, bacon, garlic, carrots and celery. Fry for about 5–10 minutes until it all starts to brown.

2. Add the thyme and the chicken and fry for another 5–10 minutes, browning the chicken slightly on both sides. Here and there the vegetables and bacon should also be turning brown in the bottom of the potjie.

3. Now add the brandy and scrape the bottom of the potjie with a wooden spoon to loosen any dark bits sticking down there. Those sticky bits create flavour but you need to scrape them loose to unleash said flavour. Let the brandy boil rapidly for a few minutes until it evaporates, then add the white wine, salt and pepper. Cover with a lid and simmer (breast sides of the chicken down) over low heat (coals, not flames) for 1½ hours. Turn the chicken breast side up for the last 15 minutes of this time.

4. Now pour in the cream, and bring back to a simmer. Cook for another 15 minutes uncovered, then remove from the fire and let the meal rest for about 10 minutes before serving.

5. Serve on mashed potatoes or white rice garnished with chopped parsley.

AND ...

If you serve it with whole sprigs of thyme, as I did for garnish in this photo, remember to move them to the side before you eat the chicken. You wouldn't eat whole sprigs of fresh thyme on your chicken as the woody parts are too hard to chew.

BASIL PESTO PASTA, WITH BRAAIED CHICKEN AND MUSHROOM

Fresh home-made basil pesto tastes great and has many uses in sandwiches, salads or pastas. It's pretty straight-forward to make, and there is a wide margin of error when adding the ingredients. Apart from the salt and pepper, you can throw in more than the indicated amount of any ingredient; then the meal will just taste more strongly of that. Braaing chicken breasts and mushrooms is also very easy, which means that you can assemble quite a fancy meal by just systematically going through some easy motions.

WHAT YOU NEED (serves 4)

For the basil pesto:

2 punnets fresh basil leaves (about 40 g)

2 cloves garlic

1 tot pine nuts (toast them in a dry pan; you could also use finely chopped cashew nuts)

2 tots Parmesan cheese (finely grated)

3 tots extra-virgin olive oil

1 tsp salt

½ tsp black pepper

For the rest:

500 g pasta of your choice

4 chicken breast fillets

250 g mushrooms (whole)

extra-virgin olive oil (for serving)

Make the pesto:

Add all the ingredients together and use a food processor or stick blender to process it to a chunky paste. If you like olive oil (like me), add more of it when you feel the urge. Taste and add a bit of salt and pepper as needed. The exact amount of salt and pepper will depend on the cheese, oil and basil you use.

You can also use an old-fashioned pestle and mortar to work the ingredients into a paste and make the pesto. If you go this route, chop the basil leaves and garlic quite finely beforehand. Also use coarse salt flakes instead of normal fine table salt to make the grinding process a bit easier.

Braai the chicken and mushrooms:

1. Put each chicken breast fillet flat on a chopping board and lightly pound the thick side with a meat mallet. You want the whole fillet uniform in thickness, and this step will make the meat easier to braai and more tender to bite.

2. Spice each chicken fillet with salt and pepper and then lightly coat them with oil. Either brush each one with oil or pour a bit of oil onto them and rub it on with your clean fingers.

3. Braai the meat for about 6–10 minutes until it is done.

4. Lightly brush the mushrooms with olive oil and then braai them at the same time that you are braaing the chicken. Either skewer the mushrooms or braai them in a braai pan with holes. Braaing mushrooms also takes about 6–10 minutes.

Assemble the pasta:

1. Cook the pasta according to the instructions on the packet. This usually involves boiling it in salted water for about 8 minutes. Drain the pasta and mix in the pesto. At this stage I usually drizzle some additional olive oil onto the mixture.

2. Slice the chicken into strips and put them and the mushrooms onto the now-green pasta. Finish the work of art with a drizzle of your best South African olive oil.

JAMAICAN JERK CHICKEN OR PORK

The fiery Jamaican braai marinade or spice known as 'jerk' is made with two key ingredients: Scotch bonnet chillies (one of the hottest chillies in the world) and allspice (pimento). If you can't find Scotch bonnet chillies, use habaneros, or any other weapon of suitable strength. Basic to jerk chicken or jerk pork is that you cook the meat over the coals of a smoky wood fire, something that we as South Africans are obviously pretty comfortable with.

If you or someone in your family knows how to use a food processor, process all of the ingredients together. Otherwise just chop the ingredients finely as mentioned below.

WHAT YOU NEED (serves 4)

about 1.3 kg chicken pieces
(or pork chops)

2 tots vegetable oil

2 tots fresh lime juice
(or lemon juice)

2 tots dark rum

3 Scotch bonnet chillies
(or habanero chillies – stemmed and finely chopped)

4 spring onions (finely chopped)

1 tot fresh garlic
(crushed or chopped)

1 tot fresh ginger
(grated or crushed)

1 tot fresh thyme
(finely chopped)

½ tot ground allspice
(allspice is also called pimento)

1 tot dark brown sugar

1 tsp salt

1 tsp black pepper

WHAT TO DO

1. Add all of the ingredients (except the meat) into a marinating bowl and mix well.

2. Add the meat and rub the marinade into the meat, making sure all pieces are coated all over. Cover the bowl and refrigerate for a few hours.

3. Remove the meat from the marinade and braai over medium coals until it is done. Pork chops will take 10–15 minutes over medium-hot coals. Chicken pieces will need a slightly higher grid to braai them and will take 20–25 minutes over medium-hot coals. Because of the marinade we're using, the meat will turn quite dark on the braai even if you're not burning it, so don't panic. Braai with care, though, as burning this marinade is a risk.

AND ...

As with any chilli, it is advisable to take care when handling the Scotch bonnet or habanero. These chillies are seriously hot and you have been warned. There is no shame in using latex gloves when preparing this recipe. Alternatively, wash your hands very well a few times before touching your eyes or any other sensitive body parts.

JAN BRAAI CHICKEN PIE

Chicken pie is part of our South African culinary heritage and, together with *bobotie* (see page 54), is a perfect way to showcase our local cuisine to visitors. For my chicken pie, you cook the filling in a potjie and braai the pastry in a hinged grid over the coals. This is a pretty special meal.

WHAT YOU NEED (serves 4–6)

1.5 kg whole chicken

1 tot olive oil

2 tsp salt

1 tsp black pepper

1 large onion (finely chopped)

3 cloves garlic
(crushed or chopped)

2 sprigs fresh thyme
(stalk off, finely chopped)

1 cup chicken stock

½ cup sherry (or white wine)

1 bay leaf

3 whole cloves

1 whole cinnamon stick

1 large potato (diced into small
cubes, about 1 cm × 1 cm)

250 g small button mush-
rooms (halved)

½ cup fresh cream
(½ a 250 ml tub)

1 packet puff pastry
(400 g, thawed)

WHAT TO DO

1. If frozen, take the puff pastry out of the freezer to thaw for later use.

2. Use a large, sharp knife to cut the chicken into 6 portions. Cut off and throw away all the skin that is easy to get off. You can leave the skin on the drumsticks for example. Make sure you cut away that triangular piece of fat that is the former tail of the former chicken.

3. Heat the oil in the potjie over a hot fire and fry the chicken portions for about 10 minutes until they are golden brown. Throw in the salt and pepper during this time.

4. Add the onion, garlic and thyme. Fry until the onions start to soften.

5. Now it's time for the stock, sherry/wine, bay leaf, cloves and cinnamon stick to go in. When the potjie starts to simmer, put the lid on and cook over a few coals for 1 hour.

6. Add the diced potato and mushrooms, then stir lightly and cook for another 30 minutes.

7. Now take the chicken pieces out of the pot and throw away the cinnamon stick. Give the chicken 15 minutes to cool down before you debone it or else your fingers will be very unhappy. While the chicken is cooling, check on the liquid in the potjie. You'll probably find it's a bit too watery, so keep the lid off and let the liquid reduce a bit, but not too much. You can fire up the potjie by adding a few more coals under it to help in this process. The second time you make this amazingly good meal, you'll know what I mean.

8. When the chicken pieces are cool enough to handle, take all the meat off the bones and throw away the skin and bones. Flake the larger pieces of meat with your fingers. Put the chicken back into the simmering pot, pour in the cream and stir well. Taste the meal before you adjust with salt and pepper as it might or might not need some.

9. When the pie filling in the potjie is nearly ready (after about an hour, at the same time as step 7, while the chicken is cooling), unroll the puff pastry from the packet. Now you have two options: either cut the pastry into the shape of the bowls you're going to serve the pies in, or cut it into squares that you will put on top of the filling on plates or in bowls. Braai the pastry shapes in an oiled, closed hinged grid for about 20 minutes over very mild coals. Turn the grid often until the pastry is golden brown and crispy. Don't braai them too fast as there is a good chance they will burn if you do. You can obviously do this step 9 at the same time as step 7 or get your braai assistant to help you out.

10. Serve by dishing up the filling into bowls or onto plates and then put the braaied pieces of pastry on top of each of them.

AND …

Chickens don't all weigh exactly the same. If you want to serve 6 people, use a slightly bigger chicken, and, if you want to serve 4, use a slightly smaller chicken.

CREOLE CHICKEN CURRY

While on holiday in Mauritius a few years ago, my brother-in-law and I used to skip the tourist traps and head to the eateries the locals favoured to eat some proper traditional Mauritian curry called *cari poule*. Although authentic Mauritian curry powder isn't readily available in South Africa, you can substitute it with any mild curry powder with added fennel and cardamom.

Remember, you need to marinate the chicken for a few hours before you start, or even overnight.

WHAT YOU NEED (serves 6)

For the marinade:

4 cloves garlic
(crushed or chopped)

1 tot fresh ginger
(crushed or chopped)

1 tot fresh thyme leaves
(finely chopped)

1 tot fresh parsley
(stems included, finely chopped)

2 tots medium curry powder

½ tot ground fennel
(just grind or pound fennel seeds)

4 cardamom pods

2 bay leaves

2 tots vegetable oil

½ cup water

For the rest of the curry:

2 kg chicken pieces
(bone in, remove skin from some of the chicken pieces or the meal will be very fatty)

1 tot vegetable oil

2 onions (chopped)

2 tins chopped tomatoes

2 tsp salt

1 tsp black pepper

fresh coriander leaves (to serve)

WHAT TO DO

1. Mix all the ingredients for the marinade together in a large marinating bowl, then add the raw chicken pieces and toss to coat on all sides. Cover and let them marinate in the fridge for a few hours, or preferably overnight.

2. Heat the oil in a potjie and fry the onions until they are soft.

3. Take the chicken pieces out of the marinade and add them to the potjie. Fry until the chicken starts to get a golden colour (don't add the rest of the marinade that is left in the bowl just yet). You don't need to cook the chicken completely; at this point you just want to give it some colour.

4. Now add the rest of the marinade and simmer over low heat for about 10 minutes.

5. Add the chopped tomatoes, salt and pepper. Bring to the boil and then simmer for 1 hour, until the chicken is tender and would start to 'fall from the bone' if you manhandled it. So work carefully, or it will actually fall off the bone. Now remove the lid and let the potjie simmer until the sauce has reduced to your liking.

6. Take the potjie off the fire and serve with white rice, topped with fresh coriander leaves – just tear them off the stalk or chop the whole lot up if you prefer.

AND ...

In my experience, you'll enjoy this curry best with a view of the sea and a side of white rum and coke. Then round it off with an afternoon nap in the shade of a tree.

CHICKEN, CAMEMBERT, FIG AND BACON BURGER

This burger is juicy, creamy, sweet and salty. It's a dream team combination and discovering it while braaing at home one evening was one of my inspirations for writing this book. It wasn't a flashing light sort of moment but it did get me thinking there's more to a braai than chops and wors. Let's emancipate the braai a bit. You can create interesting, great tasting and beautiful looking meals on the coals of a wood fire.

WHAT YOU NEED
(makes 4 burgers)

4 hamburger rolls

4 chicken breast fillets

salt and black pepper
(for seasoning)

1 tot olive oil

1 round of Camembert cheese
(sliced)

**about 8 slices of smoked
streaky bacon**

butter (to butter the rolls)

a packet of rocket leaves
(or watercress leaves)

4 ripe figs, sliced (or 4 preserved
green figs are equally good)

WHAT TO DO

1. Put each chicken breast fillet flat on a chopping board and lightly pound the thick side with a meat mallet, wine bottle, rolling pin, side of a meat cleaver or any other item of sufficient weight and size. You want the whole fillet to be uniform in thickness, and this step will make the meat easier to braai, better looking on your burger and more tender to bite.

2. Spice each chicken fillet with salt and pepper and give them a light coating of oil. Either brush each fillet with oil or pour a bit of oil into the bowl with them and toss them around until they all are coated.

3. Braai the meat for about 6–10 minutes on hot coals until it is done. The nice thing about chicken breast fillets is that you can actually see the meat colour changing from raw to ready on the braai. When you are satisfied that the chicken is almost ready and you've turned it for a final time, distribute the slices of Camembert onto the chicken breasts. You want the heat from the meat and fire to melt the cheese slightly. Now you can't turn the chicken again, as the cheese will be lost onto the coals. Take them off the fire when ready.

4. The slices of streaky bacon must be nice and crispy. The easiest and tastiest way to achieve this is on a braai grid over the coals. Lay them out carefully and only turn them once. If there's space on your grid, do this at the same time that you're braaing the chicken. Remove from the fire when ready.

5. Slice and butter the hamburger rolls and lie them buttered side down on the grid with the bacon. The idea is to lightly toast the buttered insides of the rolls. Be extra careful not to burn the rolls. Remove from the fire when ready.

6. To assemble your burger, start with the bottom half of a toasted roll, then add some rocket leaves. Next is the chicken fillet (with melted cheese), and then top that with bacon and finally the sliced figs. Cover with the top half of the toasted roll.

AND ...

You can braai the chicken, bacon and rolls at the same time, but not for the same length of time. Your aim is to have all the ingredients hot off the grid together. During the braai your two main risks are bacon strips falling through the grid onto the coals and bread rolls burning. If you're doing this meal in large quantities for a party I suggest you rope in a braai assistant or two to give you a hand.

CHICKEN THAI GREEN CURRY

A basic Thai curry sauce is quite versatile, almost like your favourite pair of braai tongs. The key ingredient is the green curry paste, and this is available at most supermarkets. Not all curry pastes are equal in strength, so if some of your friends or family members are sensitive to the odd bit of chilli in food, rather err on the side of caution when using a new green curry paste until you know what degree of ferocity you're dealing with.

WHAT YOU NEED (serves 4)

1 tot vegetable oil

1–2 tots green curry paste

3 cloves garlic
(crushed or chopped)

ginger, equal in volume to the garlic (finely chopped)

1 green chilli
(finely chopped – optional)

1 tin coconut milk (400 ml)

4 chicken breast fillets
(sliced into strips)

½ tot lemon juice (or lime juice)

salt to taste

½ cup fresh coriander leaves
(chopped)

basmati or jasmine rice (to serve, see page 182 for preparation)

WHAT TO DO

1. Heat the oil in a potjie on a medium-hot fire. Add the curry paste, garlic and ginger and fry for about 1 minute until you can smell how good it's going to taste. Watch it so that it doesn't burn, which can happen quite quickly. If you know that you and your guests like it hot, this is the time to add one or more chopped green chillies. I'm not the type of person who removes the seeds from chillies. After all, the point of adding the chillies is to add some fire to the meal. However, if you are the type of person who drinks caffeine-free coffee with fat-free milk, by all means remove the seeds.

2. Now add the coconut milk and heat it up. If anything started sticking to the bottom of the pot in step 1, use your spoon to negotiate it loose from the bottom and mix it with the rest of the sauce.

3. Add the sliced chicken breasts and boil them in the sauce for about 10 minutes. You want a medium level of boiling in the pot, so it's more than a simmer but less than a rapid boil. If your chicken is sliced thinly, it should be cooked. If your chicken is sliced thickly, cook for another few minutes. I think the easiest way to check whether the chicken pieces are cooked thoroughly is to take one of the biggest pieces and to break it open.

4. Add the lemon juice and stir well. Taste and add salt if it's needed.

5. Take the potjie off the fire and stir in the chopped coriander leaves. Serve with warm basmati or jasmine rice (see page 182) and garnish with a few extra coriander leaves.

AND ...

Once you've prepared this meal successfully, you will realise that although I used chicken here, it works just as well with beef, fish, prawns or even venison.

PERI-PERI CHICKEN LIVERS

Served with toasted bread to mop up the sauce, peri-peri chicken livers can be enjoyed as a meal on their own for breakfast, lunch or dinner. Alternatively, serve them with rice in starter portions as part of a more expansive braaied meal.

The peri-peri sauce recipe as given below can also be used with prawns, steak, fish or chicken.

WHAT YOU NEED (serves 4 people as a starter or light meal)

For the chicken livers:

1 tot oil

1 tot butter

1 onion (finely chopped)

500 g chicken livers
(completely thawed if frozen, and well rinsed and trimmed)

1 tot brandy

peri-peri sauce (see below)

½ cup cream

1 tot parsley (finely chopped)

For the peri-peri sauce:

1 tot oil

1 tot vinegar

1 tot lemon juice

1 tot water

1 tsp paprika

1 tsp chilli or peri-peri powder

1 tsp salt

2 cloves garlic
(crushed or finely chopped)

1 red chilli (finely chopped)

WHAT TO DO

1. Using a fireproof pan or cast-iron pot, heat the oil and butter.

2. Add the chopped onion and fry until soft. This takes about 4 minutes.

3. Add the chicken livers, then fry over high heat for about 5–7 minutes until they start to brown on all sides.

4. Next add the brandy and cook for another minute or two.

5. Add the peri-peri sauce and then cook for a few minutes, stirring occasionally until the sauce starts to reduce and becomes slightly sticky.

6. Now add the cream, stir, and heat through until it just starts to boil again. Take off the fire and top with chopped parsley. Serve straight from the pot, preferably with bread toasted over the coals.

Make the peri-peri sauce:

Mix together all the sauce ingredients in a bowl. Use all of this sauce in the chicken liver recipe. If the chicken livers don't taste hot enough for you, throw in some more chilli powder or chopped chillies.

AND …

You can buy chicken livers in any supermarket, usually frozen but sometimes fresh. Check the label and go for 'cleaned and trimmed' livers where you can. If you buy them frozen, first thaw them completely. Next you should clean them, if necessary, by cutting away any sinew. Lastly you should rinse them thoroughly and then drain off the excess water.

CHICKEN MAYO *BRAAIBROODJIES*

Two of my favourite meals (and I'd say this goes for most South Africans) are toasted chicken mayo sandwiches and a traditional *braaibroodjie*. Here we combine the two and create something truly awesome: a *braaibroodjie* with a chicken mayo filling. When it comes to mayonnaise, I prefer 'French style' which generally comes with a blue colour scheme on the label, to 'tangy style' whose labels are generally green – life's all about choices, so try them out for yourself. The recipe originated when I had some leftover braaied chicken and decided to employ it in this manner, but in real life you might end up having to buy rotisserie chicken now and again to prepare this feast.

WHAT YOU NEED

(for 6 *braaibroodjies*)

1 large cooked chicken
(braaied or rotisserie)

¾ cup mayonnaise

½ onion (finely chopped)

3 medium-sized gherkins
(finely chopped)

1 tot chutney

1 tot mustard (mild)

1 tot parsley (finely chopped)

½ tot milk

1 tsp salt

½ tsp black pepper

12 slices white bread

butter (for spreading on the bread)

WHAT TO DO

1. Using clean hands, take all the chicken meat off the bones. It's messy but it's not difficult. Discard the chicken bones and skin.

2. Chop or tear the deboned chicken into smaller chunks.

3. In a large mixing bowl, add all the ingredients, except the bread and butter, to the chunks of chicken and mix well.

4. Butter all the slices of bread on one side. Pack half of the slices, buttered side down, on a clean surface and then equally divide and spread all the chicken mayo filling onto them. Cover with the remaining slices (buttered side up). You now have a closed sandwich with the butter on the outside.

5. Braai the sandwiches in a hinged grid over medium coals with the grid set fairly high, turning often. The chicken is already cooked, so your only risk is burning the bread. The feast is ready when the *braaibroodjies* are golden brown and crisp on the outside.

AND ...

If you want to make this meal even more decadent, for example to serve as the main course at your wedding, you can also add some fried bacon and a slice or three of cheese to each sandwich during step 4.

TANDOORI CHICKEN

Traditional North Indian tandoori chicken is skewered and baked in a tandoor (a clay oven powered by fire). As juice drips from the meat onto the coals, the smoke adds even more flavour to the chicken – pretty similar to what happens on a braai. Skinless chicken pieces work best for this meal, as the meat can absorb the marinade better when the skin isn't in the way. A few drops of red food colouring makes little difference to the flavour but gives the meat that distinctive bright colour of 'authentic' tandoori chicken.

WHAT YOU NEED (serves 4–6)

1.5 kg chicken pieces
(like thighs and drumsticks)

4 cloves garlic (crushed)

ginger
(equal in volume to the garlic)

1 tsp ground cumin

1 tsp ground coriander

1 tot masala spice

½ tsp cayenne pepper

1 tsp salt

½ tsp black pepper

½ tot vegetable oil

½ tot lemon juice

1 cup plain yoghurt

2 drops red food colouring

WHAT TO DO

1. Prepare the chicken pieces by removing and discarding the skins.

2. In a large bowl, combine all the ingredients except the chicken and stir well. You will notice that the marinade has a pink colour; this is normal. Now add the chicken, making sure all the pieces are generously coated on all sides with marinade. You can use your recently washed hands to rub the marinade really well onto and into the meat.

3. Cover the bowl and marinate overnight in a fridge.

4. The next day, take the bowl out and bring the chicken to room temperature before braaing (it takes about 1–2 hours to lose the chill).

5. Braai over medium-hot coals in a hinged grid until the chicken is done. This should take about 20–25 minutes. Take it easy and start your grid off quite high, as the marinade might burn if the coals are too hot.

6. Serve with a salad made by mixing chopped tomatoes, cucumber and onion drizzled with lemon juice and olive oil.

AND ...

The odd black spot might appear here and there on the chicken where it over-caramelises during the braai. This is not a crisis and adds to the taste of the meal. Don't overdo it though, as there comes a point where we have to be honest and admit that it's not over-caramelised anymore, it's just plain burnt!

COQ AU VIN (CHICKEN IN WINE)

From my personal experience, this classic French dish is even better cooked in a potjie on a fire, using South African wine. The rule of thumb when cooking with wine is that you should use wine of the same quality that you drink. This doesn't necessarily mean you have to open a new great bottle of wine especially to make this potjie. It just means that if you had a braai dinner party and are left with some half-finished bottles of wine, this is exactly the meal you should cook on one of the days thereafter. You need one bottle of red wine in total, which can be a blend of more than one wine as long as they are all of a decent standard.

WHAT YOU NEED
(serves 6 hungry guests)

2 tots oil (or butter)

about 20 small pickling onions (peeled and whole)

1 carrot (chopped)

parsley equal in volume to the carrot (chopped)

4 sprigs fresh thyme

1 packet smoked streaky bacon

1 packet whole button mushrooms (about 250 g)

2½ kg chicken pieces (any mixture of thighs, legs, breasts)

1 tot cake flour

1 bottle red wine

1 tot tomato paste

2 tsp salt

2 tsp black pepper (coarse, freshly ground)

1 tot parsley (chopped)

WHAT TO DO

1. If your chicken pieces have skin on them, pull off all the skin that is easy to remove, for example on the thighs and breasts. Leave the skin on the difficult ones like drumsticks; it's definitely not worth the effort to get it off them.

2. Put your potjie over medium coals and add the oil or butter. As soon as there is heat, add the whole onions, carrot, parsley, thyme, bacon and mushrooms. Fry until the bacon starts to turn golden brown.

3. Add the chicken pieces and fry for a few minutes until they brown slightly.

4. Sprinkle the flour over everything, and stir to coat all of the chicken pieces.

5. Next add the red wine and the tomato paste, and stir well. Put the lid on the pot, and simmer for about 60 minutes until tender. Now remove the lid and let the sauce reduce until you are happy with the consistency.

6. Season to taste with salt and pepper and stir well. Take off the fire, add the chopped parsley and serve with cooked white rice (see page 182).

AND ...

Just to confirm, in case you were in any doubt, you serve this meal with red wine.

SATAY SAUCE WITH CHICKEN SOSATIES

Technically speaking this peanut-based sauce forms part of Asian cuisine, but I think of it as Dutch. Everyone I know in the Netherlands loves this stuff and if a piece of meat even so much as threatens that it was braaied, they dip it in or smother it with satay sauce. My view is that it goes best with braaied chicken sosaties.

WHAT YOU NEED

(makes about 1½ cups of sauce)

1 tot vegetable oil

1 onion (very finely chopped or even grated)

2 cloves garlic (chopped or crushed)

½ tsp chilli powder (or 2 fresh red chillies, finely chopped)

1 tot brown sugar

½ cup peanut butter (crunchy or smooth)

1 tot soy sauce

1 can coconut milk

WHAT TO DO

Make the sauce:

1. Heat the oil in a small to medium-sized potjie or pan and fry the onion, garlic and chilli until soft.

2. Next you add the brown sugar and fry until the sugar starts to caramelise.

3. Add the peanut butter and soy sauce, and stir well. Now add the coconut milk and bring to the boil while stirring until it forms a smooth sauce. Reduce the heat by dragging away some of the coals under the potjie and let the sauce simmer for about 15 minutes.

4. The satay sauce in now ready to be served with braaied chicken sosaties.

HOW TO MAKE AND BRAAI CHICKEN SOSATIES

Buy deboned chicken thighs or breasts and cut them into bite-sized chunks. Rub the meat with your favourite tailor-made braai salt (see page 152) and then skewer the meat. Cover the sosaties and leave them in your fridge until you braai them. Alternatively, just buy chicken sosaties at your favourite butchery or supermarket. Chicken sosaties made from thigh meat are juicier than those made from breast meat, so look out for those. Chicken sosaties braai in about 10 minutes over medium-hot coals and you can see the meat change in colour as it cooks.

BUTTER CHICKEN CURRY

Butter chicken is arguably the most popular of all Indian curries. Lovers of spicy food universally enjoy it, yet butter chicken is relatively mild so it suits a wide range of palates. I've met very few people in my life who don't enjoy this dish, so if you're nervously scanning through this book looking for a sure-fire winner before braaing for a tough crowd of in-laws, this is it.

WHAT YOU NEED (serves 6)

½ cup (125 g) **butter**

1 tot vegetable oil

1 onion (finely chopped)

2 cloves garlic
(crushed or chopped)

ginger paste, equal in volume to the garlic

1 tsp red chilli paste
(or 1 small red chilli, stalk off and finely chopped, or 1 tsp red chilli powder)

1 tsp turmeric

1.5 kg boneless chicken thighs
(or breasts; cut into large chunks)

2 tsp fennel seeds
(or ground fennel/barishap)

4 cardamom pods (crushed)

100 g cashew nuts
(1 packet; crush the nuts in your pestle and mortar)

1 can tomato purée
(these are normal-sized cans of about 410 g – don't confuse with tomato paste, which is the thicker one in smaller cans, nor chopped tomatoes)

1 can evaporated milk

1–2 tsp salt

½ tsp black pepper

½ cup coriander leaves
(roughly chopped; optional garnish)

WHAT TO DO

1. Add the butter and oil to your potjie and put it over a medium-hot fire. When the butter has melted, add the onion and fry for a few minutes until it starts to soften, but not brown. It might look like a lot of butter, but this is butter chicken curry after all.

2. Throw in the garlic, ginger paste, chilli and turmeric, then fry for 1 minute.

3. The chicken chunks go in next. Fry for about 5–8 minutes (depending on how hot your fire is) until the chicken starts to turn a golden brown colour on all sides.

4. Add the fennel seeds, cardamom and cashew nuts, then stir well and fry for another 1–2 minutes.

5. Pour in the tomato purée and evaporated milk, then bring to the boil and simmer for about 10 minutes until the sauce smells incredibly good and the chicken is cooked. Season well with salt and pepper, then stir for one last time and take the potjie off the fire.

6. Serve with rice (see page 182) and garnish with chopped coriander.

AND ...

Chances are your guests will really love this meal and ask you to make it again at some special occasion like your girlfriend's birthday party or your gran's bridge club AGM. For that big event, you can impress everyone by dry-toasting some extra cashew nuts in a hot pan, and topping the dish with that.

HOME-MADE MAYONNAISE, WITH BRAAIED CHICKEN AND POTATO WEDGES

There are two dishes I occasionally like to have straight up with one very simple accompaniment: mayonnaise. They are braaied chicken and potato wedges. It stands to reason, then, that you've got to use the best-quality mayonnaise – which means you'll have to make your own.

Use a stick blender if you have one; otherwise a manual whisk will do just fine and your guns (biceps) will get a workout at the same time.

WHAT YOU NEED (serves 4)

For the mayonnaise:

2 extra-large egg yolks

1 tot lemon juice

1 tsp Dijon mustard

a pinch of salt and pepper

½ cup canola oil

(Canola oil is a healthy vegetable oil that is perfect for this recipe. Sunflower and grapeseed oil also work well, as they are flavourless. You can use olive oil, but owing to its distinctive flavour your mayonnaise will end up tasting slightly different from classic mayonnaise.)

For the chicken:

2–3 chicken pieces per person

tailor-made braai salt

(see page 152)

For the potato wedges:

2 potatoes per person

olive oil

coarse sea salt flakes

WHAT TO DO

Make the mayonnaise:

1. When you use a stick blender, always remember to do the blending in a smallish upright container like a measuring jug or large plastic feta or yoghurt tub. If you don't, the mayonnaise will end up sprayed all over your kitchen. (For a manual whisk, use a large, wide mixing bowl.)

2. Add the egg yolks, lemon juice, mustard, salt and pepper to the container or bowl and using a stick blender, blend for a few seconds until well combined. (It will take about 30 seconds for manual whisking.)

3. With the motor running, add the oil in a very thin, steady stream – it takes about 2 minutes to add all the oil. The key to great mayonnaise is to add the oil really slowly. An emulsion should form to create a thick, glossy mayonnaise. (When using a manual whisk, this step should take about 6 minutes. Ask your braai assistant to pour the thin steady stream of oil while you concentrate on the whisking.)

Braai the chicken:

Make one slit with a sharp knife into the thickest part of each chicken piece. This makes it easier to braai and gets more flavour into the meat. Rub the chicken pieces with braai salt tailor-made for chicken and braai for about 20 minutes over medium-hot coals on a hinged or open grid until done.

Make the potato wedges:

I don't peel potatoes. Just wash them well and then cut each potato into four wedges. Parboil the wedges in salted water for about 10 minutes. Drain very well, i.e. get all the water off. Put them on an oven baking tray in one layer, drizzle with olive oil and give them a good sprinkle of coarse sea salt flakes. Bake until brown and crispy in an oven pre-heated to 200 °C – this will take about 30 minutes.

CHICKEN BIRYANI

This layered chicken and rice dish originated in North India but is such a firm favourite locally that we can view it as an adopted child of South African cuisine. You'll notice that I make the biryani with deboned meat. Now in that category you basically have two options – thighs or breasts. Breasts are more widely available, but thighs are less dry and have more taste, so this is the route I suggest you follow. Most supermarkets sell deboned chicken thighs these days, but if you can't find it, just use chicken breast fillets.

WHAT YOU NEED (serves 6)

2 cups basmati rice (uncooked)

2 tots butter

2 onions (finely chopped)

2 bay leaves

5 cardamom pods

1 cinnamon stick

½ tot ground turmeric

3 tots curry powder

1 tot ginger (crushed)

18–24 deboned chicken thighs
(or 8 chicken breasts fillets – cut into large chunks)

1 tsp salt

½ tsp black pepper

2 cups chicken stock

2 tots fresh coriander
(finely chopped)

almonds (flaked and toasted – optional for serving; not only tastes great but looks and sounds cool as well)

WHAT TO DO

1. Cook 2 cups of basmati rice by following the recipe on page 182. Remember, that recipe is for 1 cup, so you need to double it for this one.

2. Put your potjie on the fire. Apart from the initial frying part, this dish is made with medium-low heat all the way through, so make sure your fire is not too hot. Rather keep adding coals if the heat is not enough. Add the butter, onions, bay leaves, cardamom and cinnamon stick. Fry for about 5–10 minutes until the onions are soft and shiny but not brown.

3. Add the turmeric, curry powder and crushed ginger. Stir all of this around for another minute.

4. Now it's time for the chicken, salt and pepper to go in. Fry for about 2 minutes just to give it some colour. Pour in the chicken stock, then stir and cover with a lid. Simmer over low heat for 20 minutes, stirring half-way through.

5. Remove the lid, and top with the cooked rice, spreading it out to the edges and flattening the top. Cover with the lid, then cook for another 10 minutes over very low heat.

6. Take the potjie off the fire and leave to stand for 10 minutes before opening the lid. Serve with chopped coriander and some toasted flaked almonds.

AND ...

Chicken biryani can be slightly dry, which is just one of those things. You counteract this problem, and add to the taste, by serving it with a raita sauce, which is similar to a Greek tzatziki and is very easy to make.

Make the raita:

2 cups plain yoghurt (I prefer Greek to Bulgarian)

½ cucumber (seeds removed and coarsely grated)

1 tsp ground cumin

1 tot coriander leaves (finely chopped)

salt and pepper (to taste)

Just mix the ingredients together.

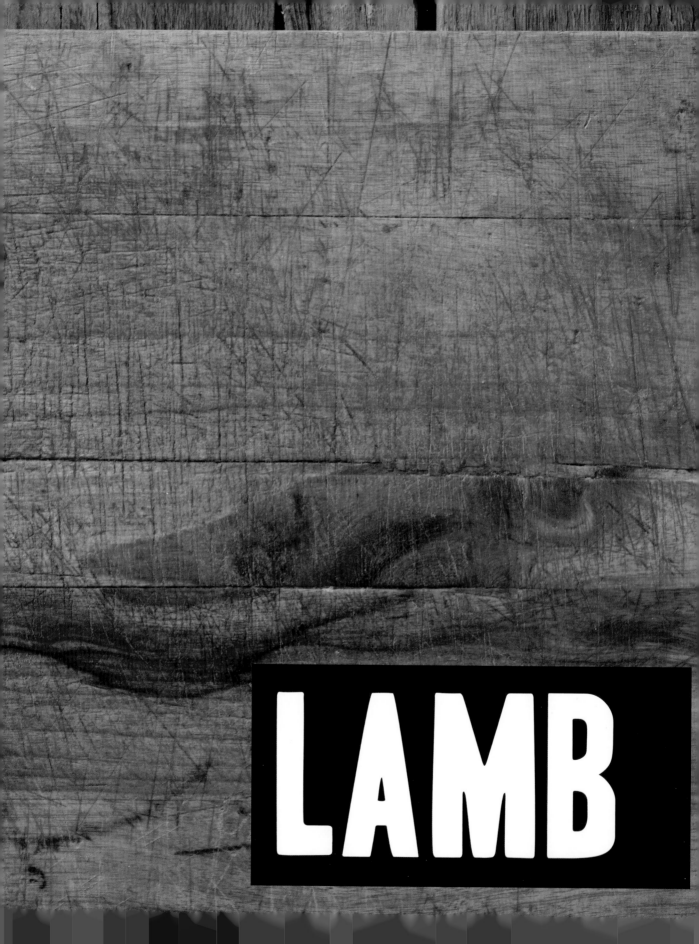

LAMB

THE LAMB LOIN CHOP IS A MEMBER OF THE BRAAI ROYAL FAMILY. I BELIEVE THAT IT SHOULD BE BRAAIED WITH CONDIMENTS LIKE OLIVE OIL, GARLIC, SALT, PEPPER, PERHAPS A BIT OF LEMON JUICE AND YOUR CHOICE OF OREGANO, THYME OR ROSEMARY. IN THIS WAY YOU WILL SIMPLY HIGHLIGHT AND NOT OVERPOWER ITS WONDERFUL YET DELICATE TASTE. IT IS WITH CHEAPER CUTS OF LAMB THAT I THINK WE SHOULD BE CREATIVE.

LAMB ROGAN JOSH

This is a superb curry with a rich and exotic flavour. Amazingly all the spices you need are available at normal South African supermarkets. Each ingredient serves a purpose in creating the aromatic end product. Take a deep breath and just follow the steps – this is one of the easier yet more impressive potjies you will make in your life; the meat doesn't even need to cook off the bone, as you're starting with deboned meat.

WHAT YOU NEED (serves 4)

2 tots vegetable oil

1 kg boneless lamb meat
(cubed – cut a leg or shoulder into cubes; alternatively I just buy enough leg chops, cut them into blocks and discard the bones)

2 onions (peeled and finely chopped)

2 bay leaves

1 cinnamon stick

6 green cardamom pods

6 whole black peppercorns

6 whole cloves
(the spice, not garlic)

6 cloves garlic
(crushed or chopped)

fresh ginger (crushed or chopped, equal in volume to the garlic)

1 tsp ground coriander

1 tsp ground cumin

1 tot paprika

1 tsp cayenne pepper

1 tsp salt

1 cup plain yoghurt

½ cup water

fresh coriander leaves
(for garnish)

WHAT TO DO

1. Heat the oil in a potjie on the fire. Add the meat cubes in batches and fry them over high heat for a few minutes until they get a nice brown colour. You will probably need two batches. Take them out of the pot and keep on a plate out of the way of dogs or hyenas. We will put the meat back in the pot later. Leave any fat or juices in the pot for the next step.

2. In the same pot, add the onions and fry for about 5 minutes until they start to soften. Add the bay leaves, cinnamon stick, cardamom pods, peppercorns and cloves, and fry for about 1 minute. Right about now you will smell some great things happening in the pot as the heat starts to release fragrances from the spices.

3. Add the garlic and ginger and stir-fry for another minute, then add the coriander, cumin, paprika, cayenne pepper and salt. Stir these in well. The mixture might be fairly dry at this point, which means things could burn, so don't have big flames under the pot. It also means you should move along quickly to the next step.

4. Put the lamb (and any juices that gathered with it on the plate) back into the potjie – it should moisten up the dry bottom. Stir right to the bottom and loosen any sticky bits with the spoon. If you're struggling, you can add a very small amount of water to help you scrape loose everything sticking to the bottom of the pot. As soon as you're done go to the next step.

5. Add the yoghurt while stirring continuously to mix it well into the dish.

6. Cook for 1–3 minutes, then add the water, and stir until you have a sauce as smooth as the Protea cricket players. Bring to the boil, then cover with a lid and gently simmer over low heat for about an hour until the meat is tender and the sauce has reduced to form a rich gravy. If your fire is too hot, the gravy will reduce too quickly and become a burnt paste, which would be a tragedy. Watch the heat carefully and stir a few drops more water into the pot if really necessary.

7. Take the pot off the fire and serve with basmati rice (see page182) and some fresh coriander leaves.

AND …

Cardamom pods are like referees in rugby matches. Without them the meal cannot exist, but they are not particularly pleasant things to encounter. They are at their best if you don't actually notice that they're there. If you spot one in the finished product, pick it out and throw it away. It has served its purpose of adding flavour to the meal.

LAMB NECK AND GREEN BEAN POTJIE (*GROENBOONTJIE BREDIE*)

You've got to know the rules to break the rules. A green bean and lamb (or mutton) potjie is older than me, and most people who will read this book; it's one of South Africa's favourite traditional combos. Cooking this dish over coals is something everyone should learn to do. As the name implies your headline-act ingredients are green beans and lamb. The potjie is relatively easy to make and doesn't contain any weird flavours so it's perfect for a diverse crowd, similar to say Merlot wine, which I suggest you serve it with.

WHAT YOU NEED (serves 6)

1 tot vegetable oil

1 kg lamb neck chops

1 tot cake flour

2 onions (finely chopped)

3½ cups beef or mutton stock

2 tsp salt

1 tsp black pepper

1 kg green beans (washed, stalks and ends removed, then sliced into chunks)

3 large potatoes (chopped into small cubes)

1 tot lemon juice

WHAT TO DO

1. Heat the oil in your potjie over a hot fire, add the meat and sprinkle the flour over it. Stir to distribute the flour all over the meat and then fry the lamb until slightly brown.

2. Add the chopped onions, and fry until the onions become soft.

3. Now add the stock, salt, pepper, beans, potatoes and lemon juice, then bring to a simmer and cook for about 2 hours until the meat is really tender and starts to fall from the bone.

4. Take off the fire and serve with rice (and Merlot).

AND …

Green beans taste best when they are fresh and in season locally. As with most fruit and vegetables, the easiest way to know whether they are in season is to check when they are very cheap. This is because they don't age well, so when they are in season there are a lot of them on the market, and the price drops. In the financial industry we call this the law of supply and demand. So in a nutshell, when you see green beans are being sold for a good price, it's your cue to make lamb and green bean potjie.

BUNNY CHOW

Culinary-wise, and I don't mean this in a negative way, the bunny chow is probably the single biggest contribution Durban in KwaZulu-Natal has made to South African society. The bunny chow is essentially curry served in a hollowed-out piece of bread loaf, and I like to use a curry made with boneless meat for it.

Although not quite Upington in the middle of summer, this curry is quite hot, so be ready for that. If you want it mild, use less chilli powder and if you're a hardened Durban curry eater, use more.

WHAT YOU NEED
(makes 4 quarter-loaf bunnies)

2 tots oil

1 onion (finely chopped)

1 tot masala (hot curry powder)

1 tsp chilli powder (optional)

500 g boneless lamb
(or mutton, cut into cubes or strips)

3 cloves garlic
(crushed or chopped)

1 tot fresh ginger
(finely chopped or grated)

1 can chopped tomatoes

2 potatoes (cut into small cubes)

2 carrots (cut into slices)

½ tot sugar

1 tsp salt

½ tsp black pepper

1 loaf fresh white bread
(you need absolutely stock-standard normal white bread, and you need it unsliced so that it can be cut to specification)

2 fresh tomatoes
(chopped, to serve)

1 punnet coriander leaves
(to serve)

WHAT TO DO

1. Heat the oil in a potjie over a medium-hot fire and fry the onion for about 5 minutes until it becomes soft. Then add the masala and (optional) chilli powder and fry for 1–2 minutes until the pan becomes sticky. If at any stage during step 1 or 2 you have too much heat in the potjie and things start to burn (in a black way, not a chilli way), add a very little bit of water as a counter-attack – but only do this if it's really necessary. We need the flavour to develop by means of getting a bit sticky at the bottom of the potjie.

2. Add the meat, garlic and ginger, and stir-fry for about 1 minute.

3. Throw in the tinned tomatoes, chopped potatoes and carrots, sugar, salt and pepper, then stir, scraping the bottom of the potjie with your spoon to loosen any and all sticky bits.

4. Cover with a lid and simmer over medium-low coals for about 30 minutes, stirring now and again so that the bottom of the potjie doesn't burn. If no amount of stirring is going to stop the dish from burning, it means your potjie is too dry. Add a bit of water to rectify this but go easy. You're making curry, not soup.

5. After 30 minutes, take off the lid and stick a fork into the potatoes to make sure they're cooked through. As soon as the potatoes are soft, the meal is essentially ready. Cook uncovered for a few minutes to allow the sauce to become a thick gravy. As soon as this happens the curry is ready, so take the potjie off the fire. Taste and adjust with a bit of extra salt if it needs it.

6. Cut the loaf of bread into quarters and then scoop or cut out the centres of each quarter loaf, essentially creating a 'bowl' of bread for the curry. You're basically creating four bowls of bread. Fill the hole of each quarter loaf with the curry and sauce. Serve the scooped out bread centre and a salad of tomato and fresh coriander leaves on the side.

SHEPHERD'S PIE

The big difference between shepherd's and cottage pie is that shepherd's pie is made with lamb or mutton, whereas cottage pie is made with beef. It's a technical thing but this is a technical book. Logic dictates that you are free to use beef instead of lamb for this recipe, but just remember to refer to the dish as cottage pie then.

For the best results use leftover braaied lamb or beef or a mix of the two. In the latter case it's called a 'shepherd's cottage pie' and it has a bit of a personality disorder, but it still tastes great.

WHAT YOU NEED (serves 6)

For the meat filling:

1 tot butter

1 onion (finely chopped)

2 medium carrots (chopped or grated)

celery equal in volume to the carrots (chopped)

1 tot cake flour

1½ cups warm beef or mutton stock

500 g braaied lamb meat (de-boned, trimmed of excess fat, and chopped; about 3 cups of chopped lamb meat)

1 tsp Worcestershire sauce

1 tsp salt

½ tsp black pepper

1 tot chopped parsley

For the mashed potato topping:

4 large potatoes

enough water for boiling the potatoes in

1 tot butter

¼ cup milk

salt and pepper

WHAT TO DO

1. In a flat-bottomed cast-iron potjie on the fire, fry the onion, carrots and celery in the butter for about 5 minutes until soft.

2. Add the cake flour and stir in before adding the warm meat stock and stirring that in.

3. Now add the meat, Worcestershire sauce, salt, pepper and parsley. Put the lid partially on the potjie (leaving a gap) and simmer gently until the sauce thickens. This can take about 45 minutes but the time will vary widely depending on a number of factors, among them how hot your fire is. During this time, do steps 4 and 5.

4. Peel the potatoes and boil them in salted water in a separate pot for about 30 minutes until they are tender. A teaspoon of salt is enough to make the water 'salted'. I really don't like peeling potatoes, and thus I usually don't. If you don't want to peel them either, then don't, but at least feel guilty about it.

5. When the potatoes are cooked, drain the water and use a potato masher to do the job it's made for. Add butter and milk to the mashed potatoes, then season with salt and black pepper and mix well. The texture should be smooth and fluffy.

6. Back to the potjie of meat on the fire: When the sauce has thickened, take off the lid and top the meat mixture with the mashed potatoes from step 5, spreading the mash into a fairly even layer to cover the surface. It's entirely acceptable if the top surface of the mash is a bit rough and not completely smooth. In fact, it's considered stylish.

7. Put the lid on the potjie and put lots of hot coals onto the lid. At this stage you don't want any heat under the pot anymore. Now bake the shepherd's pie in the potjie like that for the next 20–30 minutes until the top layer becomes slightly golden brown from the hot coals on the lid. You will obviously have to take off the lid to see whether this has happened. Don't let any ash fall into the potjie, as it won't add the kind of flavour you're looking for here. At this point the meal is ready to be enjoyed immediately.

AND ...

If you don't have any leftover braaied meat but still want to enjoy this pie, you can successfully substitute the braaied meat with 500 g fresh beef mince bought at a butcher or supermarket. Add your mince after step 1, then fry it for 5–8 minutes until it is nicely brown. Then continue with step 2 where you add the flour and stock, and follow the rest of the recipe (just ignore the part where you would 'add the meat' in step 3). It is not advisable to add uncooked mince to the potjie after the stock has been added, as the mince will then boil instead of fry, and the meal won't taste very nice.

LAMB AND TOMATO POTJIE (TOMATO *BREDIE*)

This is a very traditional recipe so your aim is to produce a meal that both your mother and mother-in-law would approve of. As the title suggests, the core ingredients are tomatoes and lamb. If you manage to find some blood-red, perhaps even slightly overripe tomatoes, and at the same time you stumble upon lamb meat on the bone, you know what to do. Any cut of lamb on the bone will do the job: neck chops or pieces of rib and shin. Supermarkets and butcheries sometimes sell packs of 'stewing lamb', which is perfect.

You will notice that no extra water or other liquid is added during the cooking process. This is because the tomatoes contain enough liquid. However, as with any other potjie, if you see that the potjie is running dry during the cooking process, add a little bit of extra water so that it doesn't burn, although I don't mention this explicitly in the method.

WHAT YOU NEED (serves 6)

2 tots vegetable oil

1.5 kg lamb cubes or pieces (some or all on bones)

½ tot cake flour

1 onion (finely chopped)

½ tot salt

1 tsp black pepper

1 kg ripe tomatoes (chopped, or 3 cans of whole or chopped tomatoes)

2 tots tomato paste

1 bay leaf

½ tot sugar

½ tot vinegar (or lemon juice)

2 large potatoes (peeled and diced into small cubes)

WHAT TO DO

1. Heat the oil in a potjie over a hot fire and then add the meat. Sprinkle the flour over the meat and stir to distribute the flour. Now fry the meat until slightly brown. This will take a few minutes, with the exact time depending on how hot your fire and pot are.

2. Add the chopped onion and fry until it becomes soft. This will take about another 5 minutes.

3. Now add salt, pepper, chopped tomatoes, tomato paste, bay leaf, sugar and vinegar, then bring to a slow simmer, cover with the lid and cook for 1½ hours until the meat starts to become tender.

4. Add the potatoes, then put the lid back on and cook for another 30 minutes until the potatoes are soft.

5. Take off the heat and serve on rice (see page 182).

AND …

About tomatoes … When a recipe like this one, and various others in this book, calls for tomatoes to be used, you have a few options. In this case, the tomato is pretty crucial to the meal, so I suggest you use real ripe tomatoes for best results. If you can't get hold of any, just use tomatoes from a tin in equal volume. When using tinned tomatoes, the ones labelled as 'whole cherry tomatoes' or 'whole and peeled' usually taste best. Just chop or mash them and add to the dish together with the juice in the tin. Failing that, use tins of chopped tomatoes. Whichever way you go, whether real tomatoes, whole from a tin or chopped from a tin, if they are not red enough and do not have a deep and rich enough tomato flavour, add extra tomato paste to rectify the problem.

WITH SEAFOOD THE RULE IS QUITE SIMPLY AS FRESH AS POSSIBLE.

SNOEK PÂTÉ

If you happen to be in possession of leftover braaied snoek, this is the best way to make use of it. Spread it on bread freshly toasted on the fire and you will outperform most smart restaurants. And, anyway, who wants to sit in a restaurant when you can stand around a fire?

WHAT YOU NEED

(serves 4–6 as a starter)

about 250 g braaied or smoked snoek (for how to braai, see *Fireworks*, page 102, and also see further comments below)

juice of half a lemon

1 tub plain cream cheese (usually about 230–250 g)

2 tots mayonnaise

½ tot parsley (finely chopped)

½ tot chives (finely chopped)

salt and black pepper

sliced bread to serve (toasted on the fire, or freshly braaied *roosterkoek*, see page 160)

WHAT TO DO

1. Remove all bones and skin from the snoek and then flake the fish thoroughly using your recently washed hands. Make sure you find and remove all the bones.

2. Put the flaked snoek in a mixing bowl along with the lemon juice, cream cheese, mayonnaise, parsley and chives. Now use a fork and mix it into a smooth and spreadable paste.

3. Taste the pâté and add salt and pepper if necessary. The amount of salt and pepper you need will obviously depend on how strongly the snoek was seasoned on the braai.

4. Spread generously on *roosterkoek* or any other freshly baked or fire-toasted bread. Enjoy around the fire with a glass of white wine in your other hand.

AND …

500 g fresh snoek yields about 250–275 g cooked flaked snoek (bones and skins removed). Fresh fish loses quite a bit of moisture on the braai. Keep that in mind when you buy fresh snoek, especially for this recipe.

If you, like me, are prone to snoek pâté cravings, you might sometimes need to make it even when you don't have leftover braaied snoek on hand. What you do then is to just buy some smoked snoek at your local fishmonger or supermarket as it also works well.

FISH CAKES

Fish cakes are packed with flavour, and as they are boneless they're also easy to eat. It's a great way to use leftover braaied fish. However, once you master this recipe you'll probably find yourself running out of leftover fish, and you'll have to braai fish from scratch to satisfy your fish cake cravings.

WHAT YOU NEED (serves 6)

1 kg braaied/cooked hake or other white fish (about 2 cups flaked boneless fish)

2 cups white bread crumbs

1 onion (peeled and grated)

1 tomato (watery seeds removed, then grated)

1 tot parsley (finely chopped)

1 tot fresh coriander (finely chopped)

1 tot fresh dill (finely chopped)

1 egg (lightly beaten)

1 tsp salt (less if your fish was seasoned during the braai)

½ tsp black pepper

2 tots vegetable oil (for frying)

fresh lemon wedges (for serving)

mayonnaise (for serving)

WHAT TO DO

1. If you are using raw fish, cook it first. The easiest way would be to quickly braai it over hot coals, or to panfry it in a little oil. This should not take more than 15 minutes.

2. With clean hands, flake the cooked fish (make sure you get rid of all the bones) and then combine with all the other ingredients (except the oil and lemon wedges) in a mixing bowl. Mix well.

3. Shape the mixture into golf ball-size portions, flatten them slightly and put them on a tray. If you don't want your tray to smell fishy afterwards, first cover it with a sheet of baking paper.

4. Over a medium-hot fire, heat the oil in a large flat-bottomed cast-iron pot or fireproof pan. Fry the fish cakes in batches on both sides, turning each one only once. When they are golden brown on both sides, they are ready. This should take about 5–8 minutes. This is not a difficult task and can be outsourced to someone who asks 'how can I help?'

5. As you take them out of the pan, place the fish cakes on a couple of sheets of kitchen paper to absorb any extra oil. Then plate and serve with mayonnaise, lemon wedges and a fresh green salad.

AND ...

You can use any edible fish for this recipe, and your choice of fish will obviously decide the flavour of the fish cakes. Hake works well, but if you're feeling royal use salmon or trout. If you're on a camping trip in the middle of Africa, tinned tuna is the way to go.

SEAFOOD POTJIE

The quality of the seafood you use here will have a direct impact on the taste and texture of the end result, so use fresh seafood as far as possible. Not all frozen seafood is bad (I use frozen prawns often) but in South Africa we can get plenty of fresh fish and mussels, and that's why I prefer using fresh stuff.

    The great thing about a seafood potjie is that you don't need to start cooking it hours in advance, as it only takes about 30 minutes – it's much quicker than making meat potjies. The only thing that takes a bit of time is preparing your fresh seafood.

WHAT YOU NEED (serves 6–8)

2 tots olive oil

1 onion (finely chopped)

2 celery sticks (finely chopped)

1 large carrot (grated or finely chopped)

5 cloves garlic (crushed or chopped)

1 bottle dry white wine

2 cups fish stock (or chicken stock)

1 kg black mussels (cleaned and washed)

1 kg prawns (in the shell, digestive tracts removed)

700 g–1 kg white fish fillets (skinless and boneless, cut into bite-size cubes)

1 cup cream (250 ml tub)

1 tot cornflour

2 tsp salt

1 tsp black pepper

1 tot lemon juice

2 tots parsley (finely chopped)

PREPARE THE SEAFOOD

Mussels: Clean the mussels by scrubbing them with a brush, and then remove the beard by pulling it towards the narrow tip of the mussel until it breaks out. Rinse the mussels thoroughly and leave them in a bucket of fresh water for an hour. During this time, stir the mussels once or twice so they all get a chance to be exposed to the fresh water. If there is a lot of sand at the bottom of the bucket, replace the water. Discard all mussels that are open, floating or have cracked shells. At the end of the hour, wash the mussels again in clean water. Remember, sand is the enemy so it's even better if you can leave them in fresh water for 2 hours.

Prawns: Using a pair of sharp kitchen scissors, cut the back of the prawn open from the gap just behind the head to the tail. Gently lift and pull out the digestive tract with the tine of a fork. See bottom of page 112 for more on this topic.

Fish: If you know how to do it, fillet your fish and remove the bones with tweezers. Then carefully take off the skin and slice into bite-size cubes. Otherwise ask your fishmonger or a fisherman friend to do the job for you.

WHAT TO DO

1. Heat the potjie over a hot fire, add the olive oil and then fry the onion, celery, carrot and garlic for 5–10 minutes until soft, but not too dark.

2. Now add the wine and stock, and bring to the boil.

3. Drop the mussels into the potjie, then layer the prawns and fish cubes on top. Put the lid on and simmer gently for about 15 minutes. In the meantime, mix the cream with the cornflour (this is a trick I learnt from Carmen Niehaus).

4. Once the fish starts to look cooked, add the cream and cornflour mixture, as well as the salt, pepper and lemon juice. Stir everything in the potjie together very gently, or else the fish will flake and fall apart. Heat until warm and let the mixture simmer for a further 5–10 minutes until the sauce begins to thicken. Remove the pot from the fire and add the chopped parsley.

5. Serve with rice, or even with bread.

SEARED TUNA WITH SESAME SEEDS

As with any fish you want to braai, the most important thing is to make sure the tuna is fresh. The only way to do that is to buy it from a trusted, reputable fishmonger who can tell you exactly where he or she got the tuna from, and when it was caught. If you're unsure about the freshness of the tuna, don't buy it. Needless to say, the other sure-fire way to get fresh tuna is to catch it yourself.

WHAT YOU NEED (serves 4)

4 tuna steaks of about 200 g each (very fresh or 'sashimi grade')

1 tot vegetable oil

salt and black pepper

about ½ cup sesame seeds (bonus points for a mixture of black and white if you can find it)

½ cup good-quality soy sauce

1 tot ginger (grated or crushed)

1 spring onion (finely sliced)

½ tot sugar

½ tot white vinegar

WHAT TO DO

1. Lie the tuna steaks in a dish, then brush them lightly with oil, and season with salt and pepper on both sides. Leave them in a cool place but out of the fridge for 10 minutes so they reach room temperature. Don't leave them too long before cooking, as fish can go off quickly.

2. Put the sesame seeds in another dish or on a plate and then dip the steaks on all sides into the sesame seeds to coat them evenly.

3. Carefully (so that the sesame seeds don't fall off) put the tuna steaks in a clean hinged grid, then braai them over very hot coals for about 1 minute each on both sides. If you're wondering whether your coals are hot enough, then they aren't! Take the steaks off the fire and put them on a wooden board to cool for 5–10 minutes before you slice them.

4. While the tuna is resting, mix the soy sauce, ginger, spring onion, sugar and vinegar together in a bowl or jug, stirring until the sugar has dissolved.

5. Use a very sharp knife and cut the tuna steaks into slices. If you don't have a very sharp knife, buy a new knife, use a knife sharpener, or both. As you will notice from the photo on the opposite page, the fish is still raw in the middle. This is supposed to be the case with seared tuna. After all, that same piece of fish could be served as completely raw sashimi in a restaurant.

6. Drizzle the sauce over the fish, or serve the sauce in small dipping bowls on each plate.

AND ...

Only braai sustainably sourced fish – so stay away from something like bluefin tuna or anything else floating around on the SASSI red list.

TROUT FILLETS WITH DILL BUTTER

Unlike salmon, which are too lazy to swim to South Africa and have to be flown here, trout has made its way to South African waters. If you, like me, have tried to master the art of fly fishing but failed miserably, don't despair – you can buy fresh trout at various trout farms in the Western Cape, Mpumalanga escarpment and Drakensberg areas. You can also get it at most good supermarkets and fish shops. The trout fillets you buy are usually pin-boned already (in other words without bones). If not, ask your fishmonger to do it for you. Trout is great on the braai, as the smoke from the coals and fire adds a delicious flavour to it. There's no reason to cook it any other way.

WHAT YOU NEED (serves 4)

½ cup butter (melted)

1 tot fresh dill (chopped)

1 clove garlic
(finely chopped or crushed)

½ tot smooth apricot jam

juice of half a lemon

salt and pepper

1 kg fresh trout fillets

WHAT TO DO

1. Mix the melted butter, dill, garlic, apricot jam and lemon juice in a cup or mug.

2. Wash the trout fillets under cold running water and then pat them dry with paper towels. Put the fish fillets on a hinged grid, skin side down. You could first brush the skin side lightly with oil so that it doesn't stick to the grid. Brush the flesh side generously with the butter sauce.

3. Braai the fillets on a hot fire, skin side down first, for about 5 minutes. Turn the grid, and braai the flesh side for another 5 minutes. By now the fish should be cooked through and should flake easily. Depending on the thickness of the fillets, the braai time could be shorter, especially if you like your trout a bit pink in the middle.

4. Take the grid off the fire and brush the trout once more with the butter sauce. Now carefully take the fish off the grid. Sometimes the fish comes away from the skin as you do this, and that's fine because you're not going to eat the skin anyway. Serve at once, adding salt and pepper to taste.

AND ...

Serve with potato wedges (see page 84 for how to make them) and salad.

PRAWN THAI RED CURRY

This is one of those meals that you used to order at a restaurant as it was your only way to get hold of something you love. But then you learnt that it's not only easy to make, but also tastes better at home. Why? – because you control all the inputs. The basic Thai red curry sauce works well with any seafood, so you can replace the prawns in this recipe with white fish fillets. The preparation method for all Thai curry sauces is similar, so once you've mastered this one, why not make some chicken Thai green curry as well (see page 70).

WHAT YOU NEED (serves 3)

1 tot vegetable oil

1–2 tots Thai red curry paste
(available in most supermarkets)

3 cloves garlic
(crushed or chopped)

ginger, equal in volume to the garlic (finely chopped)

1 red chilli
(finely chopped – optional)

1 tin coconut milk (400 ml)

1 tsp Thai fish sauce

500 g whole prawns

juice of half a lemon (or lime)

salt to taste

½ cup fresh coriander leaves
(chopped)

basmati or jasmine rice
(to serve; see page 182 for preparation)

fresh coriander leaves
(extra, to garnish)

WHAT TO DO

1. Prepare the prawns as described at the bottom of this page.

2. Heat the oil in a potjie on a medium-hot fire. Add the curry paste, garlic and ginger and fry for about 1 minute until you can smell how good it's going to taste. Watch it so that it doesn't burn, which can happen quite quickly. If you know that you and your guests like it hot, this is the time to chuck in one or more chopped red chillies.

3. Now add the coconut milk and fish sauce and heat it up. If anything started sticking to the bottom of the pot in step 1, use your spoon to loosen it and mix in with the rest of the sauce.

4. Throw in the prawns and 'poach' or simmer them in the sauce for about 10 minutes until they are cooked – they will turn a bright orange colour. Add the lemon/lime juice, stir well and season with salt to taste.

5. Take the pot off the fire and stir in the chopped coriander leaves.

6. Serve with warm basmati or jasmine rice and garnish with extra coriander leaves.

HOW TO PREPARE PRAWNS FOR USE IN CURRY

In South Africa, you usually buy frozen prawns. Thaw the prawns by putting them in a bowl of cold (normal tap) water for 30 minutes. You want to cook them with the head on, as this gives extra flavour, but you need to get that vein out of the tail. Using a pair of sharp kitchen scissors, cut the back of the prawn open from the gap just behind the head to the tail. Gently lift and pull out the digestive tract with the tine of a fork.

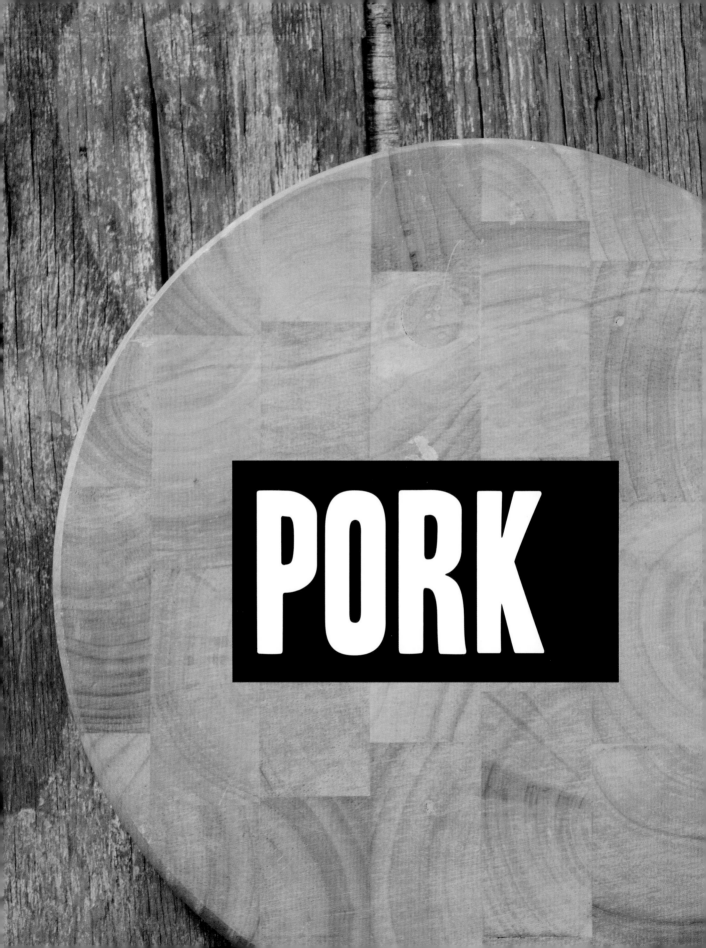

PORK SHOULD NEVER REALLY BE SERVED BEFORE BEING INFUSED WITH THE SMOKY FLAVOUR OF A FIRE.

PORK CHOPS WITH PLUM SAUCE

It's usually a good idea to serve pork loin chops with sauce, as they have a general tendency to be a bit dry, even if you braai them correctly. Plum sauce is easy to make and superb with pork, which makes these two a perfect match.

WHAT YOU NEED

(makes enough sauce to serve at least 8 people)

2 tots butter

2 onions (finely chopped)

500 g plums (halved and stoned)

1 cinnamon stick

1 star anise (whole)

2 cloves

2 cups red wine

½–1 cup sugar (depends how sweet your plums are)

1 tsp salt

½ tsp black pepper

pork loin chops (2 per person)

WHAT TO DO

Make the sauce:

1. Heat the butter in a potjie, then add the onions and fry slowly until they are very soft and shiny but not brown.

2. Add the plums, cinnamon stick, star anise, cloves, wine, sugar, salt and pepper, then simmer (covered) over medium-low heat for about 1 hour, stirring every 10–15 minutes. The plums should disintegrate completely and form a thick sauce. Watch the fire carefully as the potjie will cook dry if the heat is too intense. Low heat is the way to go. You can, for example, make this sauce while watching rugby, then you can go and stir the sauce every time there is a scrum that keeps on collapsing.

3. After 1 hour of simmering, remove the sauce from the fire and cover with a lid until you're ready to eat. You don't need to serve the sauce hot, so you can let it cool down to room temperature before or during the braai, depending on circumstances.

Braai the pork chops:

1. If it bothers you, cut away the excess fat running along the side of each chop but leave at least a thin and even fat layer.

2. Rub the chops with your own special brand of braai salt (see page 152) or season with salt and pepper, cover, and let them rest in the fridge until you're ready to braai.

3. Put the chops on the grid and braai on hot coals, turning often, for about 12 minutes in total until they're done medium.

4. Pork loin chops should always be served medium. When you cut a pork chop on your plate, only clear juices should run out; no pink or red. An internal temperature of 70 °C in the thickest parts equates to medium – so use your meat thermometer to be sure.

SCHWEINSHAXE (BRAAIED PORK KNUCKLES)

Schweinshaxe is a German dish, famous the world over. You start off by cooking pork hocks or eisbein until they are very tender. Then you braai them over hot coals to give them a great flavour and make them crispy. This tastes far superior to the classic German version where you just grill them in an oven to finish them off.

If your butcher or supermarket only has smoked pork hocks or smoked eisbein, don't worry; it works just as well and obviously your meal will have an even deeper smoky flavour.

WHAT YOU NEED (serves 4)

4 small pork hocks or eisbeins
(regular or smoked)

2 bottles apple cider
(like Hunters or Savanna)

2 cups water

salt

WHAT TO DO

1. Put everything into a large potjie. The liquid should just cover the pork, so add extra water if necessary.

2. Put the potjie over a hot fire, then cover with a lid and bring to the boil. Simmer (it mustn't boil rapidly) for 2½–3 hours, then take it off the fire. You want the meat nice and soft but not falling off the bone. You should check on the meat during this time as it might be ready sooner; this is not an exact science.

3. Use braai tongs to lift the cooked pork hocks out of the potjie, shake off the liquid and then generously salt them (smoked hocks will generally be very salty already, and will not need any extra salt).

4. Now for the braai: You'll need an open grid as a hinged grid won't close over the hocks. Braai for about 20 minutes in total over hot coals until they are nicely browned on all sides. Remember, the meat is already cooked so you just want to give it some crunch, colour and flavour.

5. Serve immediately with boiled or mashed potatoes, coleslaw (see page 156) and mustard.

AND ...

If your pork is cooked before you're ready to braai, take the potjie off the coals and let the hocks rest in the water – an hour or two of resting in lukewarm water will just result in more tender pork.

During the photo shoot for this book, we figured out that painting the meat with honey during the final stages of the braai not only gives it a great colour and shine, but also a very luxurious taste. Give it a go!

PORK SPARERIBS WITH FENNEL AND CHILLI

Pork, fennel and chilli are great friends. You can use this combination of spices on pretty much any cut of pork you're going to braai, but the nice thing about spareribs is that they have a high content of bone and fat. Both of these will give extra flavour to the meat as it heats up during the fairly lengthy braai time.

In this recipe, you're using a dry rub and you're aiming for ribs with a crisp spicy crust. If you're looking for the ultimate sweet and sticky pork ribs, find the sparerib recipe in *Jan Braai – Fireworks*.

WHAT YOU NEED (serves 6)

2.5 kg pork spareribs or loin ribs (in whole racks)

1 tot olive oil

1 tot dried chilli flakes

1 tot fennel seeds

1 tot salt flakes
(or medium-coarse salt)

1 tsp freshly ground black pepper

WHAT TO DO

1. Rub a thin coating of oil all over the ribs.

2. Put the chilli flakes, fennel seeds, salt and pepper in a pestle and mortar, then pound it to a coarse texture (you don't want it fine). Season the ribs all over with the spice mixture.

3. Over medium-hot coals, and the grid set relatively high, braai the ribs for about 1 hour, turning quite often. Your braai assistant can tend to your needs during this time while you tend to the meat's needs. The ribs should be a deep golden brown and the meat should be tender and start to pull away from the bones. If the ribs were quite thin and the heat quite high, they might be ready after 40 minutes.

4. Take them off the fire and cut into riblets with a sharp knife. Don't cut in the middle of the strips of meat. You cut ribs as close to the bone as possible, so that each riblet has bone on one side, and a good thick piece of meat on the other. This just makes them easier to eat. If the riblets still look a bit raw in the middle, this is absolutely no crisis at all; in fact it's an opportunity to add more flavour. Put them back on the grid and braai the exposed cut parts of meat for a few minutes until the meat is done.

5. Ribs are best enjoyed by hand, so you can serve them straight from the cutting board or a bowl. When you eat like this around the fire, don't throw the empty bones into the coals though, as that creates an unsavoury smell.

AND ...

For a special occasion (like a braai) you can serve these ribs with home-made sweet chilli sauce (see page 22), which should not be confused with its infinitely inferior shop-bought counterpart.

CURRIED PORK NECK CHOPS

When I asked my father which meals he would definitely put in this book, the first one he mentioned was curried pork neck chops. It is one of those definitive and original South African braai meals.

When braaing pork, neck chops are generally your best bet as they are quite tender, and have some marbling so they won't dry out too quickly. If you leave them in this curry marinade for a few hours before the braai, it will not only create a great taste but will also make them even more tender and juicy. As with all pork dishes, these chops should be braaied until their internal temperature is 70 °C, so use your meat thermometer to measure that.

WHAT YOU NEED (serves 6)

12 pork neck chops

2 tots oil

1 onion (finely chopped)

2 cloves garlic (finely chopped)

1 tot fresh ginger
(crushed or finely grated)

1 tot curry powder (if, like me, you like a bit of burn, use medium or hot curry powder, but, if your tongue is easily offended by a chilli, use mild curry powder)

1 tsp turmeric

1 cup brown vinegar

1 cup smooth apricot jam

1 tsp salt

½ tsp black pepper

WHAT TO DO

1. Heat the oil in a medium-sized pot over high heat, then add the onion. Fry until the onion becomes soft and shiny, then add the garlic and ginger and fry for another 2 minutes. You can prepare the marinade on a stove or fire as you see fit.

2. The curry powder and turmeric go in next. Fry for 1 minute, stirring well.

3. Add the vinegar and apricot jam, then bring to the boil. Scrape the bottom to loosen any sticky bits. Cook for 5 minutes.

4. Add the salt and pepper, and stir well. Take the marinade off the heat and let cool for an hour or two until the marinade is at room temperature.

5. Pour the curry marinade over the pork neck chops, which you should have in a marinating bowl. Mix it in and make sure that the marinade is in contact with all parts of the meat. Cover and marinate for 3–4 hours (if it is very hot outside, marinate in the fridge).

6. Take the chops out of the marinade and shake off any excess sauce. Braai over a hot fire for about 5–7 minutes a side, depending on the size of the chops. Use your meat thermometer to check that they're ready.

ASIAN-STYLE PORK BELLY

Pork belly used to be something I liked to order at fancy restaurants. But then I figured out how to braai it, which, not surprisingly, makes it taste even better. The meat looks quite fatty and tough to start with, but after 2 hours of steady heat most of that fat braais out, and the meat gets very tender.

Basically, you're going to braise the meat with an amazing smelling Asian-style marinade inside your man-oven. The result will be a succulent piece of pork with a crispy, smoky outer layer of fat called crackling. Guaranteed you and everyone else will love it.

WHAT YOU NEED (serves 4)

1 cup soy sauce

1 cup orange juice

peeled rind of 1 orange
(solid peel, not grated or zested)

1–2 cups chicken stock

1 whole star anise

1 cinnamon stick

1 tot chopped fresh ginger

½ cup brown sugar

1 kg pork belly
(ask your butcher for one with a relatively thin layer of fat)

WHAT TO DO

1. Load your man-oven with enough charcoal so that you can braai for 2 hours using the indirect method, and light the fire.

2. Score the fat. This means you must use a sharp knife to cut a criss-cross pattern into the outer layer of fat.

3. In a flameproof roasting tray (about 5 cm deep), which is large enough to fit your pork belly snugly, throw in all the ingredients except the meat. Stir well to dissolve the sugar slightly.

4. Now add the pork belly fat side up, and spoon some of the marinade over the top. The liquid should come up the sides but not completely cover the top of the meat.

5. Put the roasting tray inside the man-oven (on the top grid), then close it and regulate the temperature with the top and bottom valves. Cook at 150 °C for about 2 hours, until the top is brown and crispy and the meat is very tender. Half-way during the cooking process you can open the man-oven once to spoon more of the sauce in the roasting tray onto the meat. Remember that opening the man-oven lets lots of the heat escape, so only do it once and do it quickly. If you're worried there might not be enough heat, rather don't open it at all.

6. Take the tray out of the man-oven and remove the meat from the tray. Put the meat on a wooden cutting board and let it rest for a few minutes. If you like, you can use the sauce left in the roasting tray to make a serving sauce (see below). Slice the meat into 2 cm-thick slices and serve with mashed potatoes and any other vegetables you have on hand.

AND ...

If you prefer the top of your belly even crunchier, braai the belly with the fat side down over direct coals at the end of the cooking time.

Make a serving sauce with leftover roasting liquids:

Put the liquid into a pot, and give it a taste – if it has reduced too much and the flavour is too strong, just add a few tots of chicken stock or water, then bring to the boil. Mix half a tot of cornflower and half a tot of cold water in a cup, then add a little of the roasting liquid to create a paste. Stir this paste slowly into the boiling sauce. It should thicken up instantly. Remove from the heat and serve with the meat.

OSTRICH& VENISON

VENISON IS NATURALLY QUITE A LEAN MEAT AS THE ANIMALS WERE RUNNING AROUND IN THE VELD ALL DAY. IF FREE-RANGE MEAT IS YOUR THING, LOOK NO FURTHER.

OSTRICH FILLET SALAD

Ostrich meat is quite South African. It's also quite healthy. While we're on the healthy route, I suggest serving ostrich fillet in the form of a salad. As with beef steak, you braai ostrich fillet over very hot coals. Let it rest properly before slicing it into thin slivers. These days you can find vacuum-packed ostrich fillets on the meat counters of almost any supermarket in the country.

WHAT YOU NEED (serves 4)

800 g ostrich fillets

2 tots olive oil

salt and pepper

6 nectarines (or peaches – perfectly ripe, stoned and halved)

1 large bag fresh rocket leaves (or watercress)

3 rounds feta cheese (about 200 g)

olive oil (for drizzling)

balsamic reduction (or vinegar, for drizzling)

WHAT TO DO

1. Splash the olive oil over the ostrich fillets and toss them around so that they are coated with oil on all sides. Now season them all over with salt and pepper.

2. Use a brush or your recently washed hands to also coat the cut side of the nectarine halves with olive oil.

3. Over a very hot fire, braai the fillets for 4–5 minutes a side, then take them off the heat and let them rest for at least 10 minutes. (The idea here is not that you have to serve the meat while it is still hot from the fire. The idea is that you serve meat that has a great flavour from the fact that it was braaied.) Ostrich meat can be enjoyed medium rare, but you can also braai it medium with an internal temperature of 70 °C. I wouldn't braai it past that point, as it will then just become dry and tasteless.

4. On less heat (set the grid higher and/or scrape away some coals), braai the nectarines cut side down for about 2 minutes, just to give them some colour.

5. Slice the fillets into very thin slivers, showing off the pink insides. For this you'll need a very sharp knife so, if you don't have one yet, buy a knife sharpener or new knife or both. Now put the salad together using all of the other ingredients. Finish with a drizzle of some olive oil and balsamic reduction or balsamic vinegar.

AND ...

For a special day, say for example Valentine's Day, substitute the nectarines/peaches with strawberries, as they also go well with braaied ostrich. If on any normal day you can't get hold of ostrich fillet for this recipe, just use normal beef fillet and braai it medium rare.

VENISON SOSATIES

This is a great way to braai your venison. The marinade adds some bite and sweetness, and the long marinating time not only tenderises the meat but also makes it juicier. Before the braai you skewer the meat with dried fruit and bacon. All this contributes to a truly great sosatie. I got this recipe from a man by the name of Stephen in Bela-Bela, where he has a butchery that specialises in venison, and naturally he knows his stuff when it comes to braaing this type of meat.

WHAT YOU NEED (serves 8)

For the marinade:

1 tot oil

2 onions (chopped)

1 tot medium curry powder

1 tsp turmeric

1 cup normal brown vinegar

450 g can smooth apricot jam

1 standard-sized bottle of chutney

8 allspice berries

3 cloves

½ tot salt

1 whole cinnamon stick

For assembling the sosaties:

2 kg boneless venison
(kudu, gemsbok, springbok, etc., cut into chunks)

250 g dried peaches

250 g dried apricots

1 pack of bacon (cut into squares)

WHAT TO DO

1. Fry the onions in the oil for a few minutes in a potjie (on the fire) or pot (on the stove) and then add all the other marinade ingredients. Stir well, bring to the boil and let simmer for 10 minutes.

2. Take the marinade off the fire or stove and let it cool down. Put it in a marinating bowl, then add the chunks of meat to it. Cover and let it marinate in the fridge for at least 12 hours, but preferably for 2 or 3 days. Toss the meat every 8–12 hours to ensure all sides of the meat get proper exposure to the marinade.

3. Assemble the sosaties by skewering chunks of meat with pieces of bacon, dried peaches and dried apricots.

4. Braai the sosaties for about 12 minutes on medium-hot coals with your grid relatively high. The sugar in the marinade as well as the sugar in the peaches and apricots can burn quickly, so take it easy on the heat. We're not braaing steak.

KLEIN KAROO OSTRICH BURGER

On the R62 road in the Klein Karoo lie three towns in a row, perfectly positioned for a regional dish. As you drive from Cape Town, the first one you pass through is Ladismith with its cheese factory. Next you get Calitzdorp, known for its port, and, lastly, there is Oudtshoorn, a town steeped in a rich ostrich heritage.

WHAT YOU NEED
(serves 2 hungry people)

1 onion

1 tot butter

1 cup Cape Ruby Port

4 ostrich patties
(500 g packet, widely available at leading supermarkets)

2 hamburger rolls

lettuce

tomato (sliced)

100 g cheese
(aged for 3–6 months; grated)

2 sprigs rosemary

WHAT TO DO

1. Slice the onions into rings and sauté them with the butter. To sauté means to lightly fry in a pan. This will take about 5 minutes.

2. Add the port and reduce until the port is completely absorbed into the onions and it becomes a sticky, dark purple relish. Keep to one side.

3. Paint the patties with olive oil and braai for 6–8 minutes over hot coals until they are cooked medium.

4. Butter the rolls and toast their insides on the braai grid during the final 1 or 2 minutes of the braai.

5. Assemble the burger in this order: bottom half of roll, lettuce, tomato slices, ostrich patty, grated cheese, another patty, onions, top half of roll. Keep it together by inserting a rosemary sprig with all its leaves removed, except for the top few (or failing that a sosatie stick) through the middle of the burger from top to bottom.

LEG OF VENISON IN PORT

Venison goes very well with sweeter ingredients like dried fruit and port. Instead of trying to choose between the two, I like to just add both. This creates a truly legendary dish with a cut of meat that can otherwise be difficult to cook and which can easily end up dry.

WHAT YOU NEED (serves 8)

Stage 1:

2 kg leg of venison
(bone in – make sure it will fit into your potjie, otherwise ask your butcher to cut it into two pieces)

½ tot ground coriander

1 tot chopped rosemary

5 whole cloves

1 whole cinnamon stick

3 bay leaves

1 bottle port

about 10–12 garlic cloves (whole)

Stage 2:

2 tots oil

2 onions (chopped)

1 packet bacon (chopped)

3 carrots (peeled and sliced)

250 g mixed dried fruit
(apricots, apples, prunes, etc.)

2 tots lemon juice

2 tsp salt

1 tsp black pepper

WHAT TO DO

Stage 1:

1. Mix the coriander, rosemary, cloves, cinnamon stick, bay leaves, port and garlic in a bowl.

2. Now let the meat and marinade join forces either in a large marinating bowl (plastic, glass or ceramic) or a plastic bag. Cover the bowl or seal the bag and let it marinate in a fridge for 2 days. Turn the meat roughly every 8–12 hours.

Stage 2:

1. Take the meat out of the fridge an hour before you start cooking.

2. While the potjie heats up over your fire, take the meat out of the marinade and quickly 'flame-grill' it over very hot flames for about 3 minutes a side to give it a nice colour (don't throw the marinade away; keep it for later). Take the meat off the fire and keep it out the way of hyenas, dogs, etc.

3. Over a hot fire, heat the oil in the potjie and fry the onions and bacon for a few minutes until the onions are soft and start to brown.

4. Put the browned meat inside the potjie, and then add all the marinade left in your marinating bowl or bag. Heat up till the sauce starts simmering, then cover with the lid and cook over a low fire for 2 hours. It should just be a slow simmer.

5. If prunes are one of the dried fruits you want to add, now is the time to pit them if they don't come that way in the packet. Otherwise it's a broken tooth waiting to happen and that's no fun when you're camping in the bush.

6. After 2 hours of simmering, add the carrots, dried fruit, lemon juice, salt and pepper, and then simmer for a further 1 hour (covered). Keep the temperature low and steady. Add a bit of water only if the pot looks too dry.

7. By now the meat should be really tender. Lift the meat out of the pot onto a wooden carving board and slice into thick chunks – it should just about fall apart by itself.

8. Put the meat chunks back in the pot and stir them carefully into the sauce. Add more salt if necessary. Serve with mashed potatoes. It will be great – end of story.

AND ...

If you want more sauce in your pot after carving the meat into chunks (before adding the meat back into the pot), just add a cup of beef stock to the sauce in the pot and bring it to the boil. Boil for about 2 minutes, then thicken slightly with some dissolved cornflour if necessary (mix half a tot each of cornflour and water, see instructions at the bottm of page 124). Stir and bring to a simmer, then add the meat to the sauce and serve.

OTHER AWESOME STUFF

EVERYTHING TASTES BETTER WHEN IT'S BRAAIED.

STOKBROOD

As you've noticed by now, I don't think braaing has to be limited to things on grids. We can also do it in potjies and pans or, as in this case, on a stick. Braaing *stokbrood* is a great family activity. When I was young we used to do it all the time while camping in the Cederberg. Not only does it keep your kids busy, but it also introduces them to some basic principles of braaing: using gentle heat and turning often so that the inside is done before the outside burns. My favourite fillings for *stokbrood* are freshly braaied boerewors (in my first one) and butter and golden syrup (in the second one).

WHAT YOU NEED (makes 8–10)

1 kg cake flour

10 g instant yeast
(1 small packet)

1 tot sugar

½ tot salt

about 2½ cups water
(slightly warm)

2 tots olive oil

washed wooden sticks
(the thickness of a broomstick)

WHAT TO DO

1. Throw the flour, yeast, sugar and salt into a very large mixing bowl and mix well with one of your recently washed hands.

2. Add the oil and just more than 2 cups of water (I usually need about 550–600 ml) and mix well with your hands to form a soft dough. Start with 2 cups, and then add a little more water if the mixture is too dry. Continue to mix until the dough comes together as a ball.

3. Move this dough ball to a clean flat surface (wooden board, table top, kitchen counter, bonnet of your bakkie) and knead for about 5 minutes until the dough is smooth, elastic and in one pliable piece. Don't add any extra flour unless the dough is really very sticky – you'll see the texture usually changes quite rapidly from sticky to elastic while you're kneading it.

4. Put the dough back in the mixing bowl and cover it with a damp kitchen towel or plastic wrap. Leave it for about 30 minutes to rise until it is about double in volume.

5. When ready, turn the dough out onto a lightly floured surface (wooden board, table top, kitchen counter, bonnet of your bakkie), then knead for a few strokes, just to punch out some of the air (as the Springbok front row does when scrumming against the Australians).

6. Divide the dough into 8–10 pieces and then roll out each piece into a long strip of around 30–40 cm.

7. Start at the one end of a stick and attach the end of a piece of dough onto it. Press it slightly so that it can't come loose too easily. Now roll the dough around the stick from the top, until you get to the end of the piece of dough. Tuck in the end to make sure it doesn't come loose. (If you don't have enough sticks, just do this and the next part in batches.)

8. You can now proceed to braai the *stokbrood* or you can leave the rolled coils of dough on the sticks in a upright position for a few minutes to rise again. Over medium-hot coals and turning often, braai the *stokbrood* for about 15 minutes until it has a nice brown shine. If your arms get tired, there are all sorts of creative ways involving kids or rocks to make your *stokbrood* stand on its own.

9. When the *stokbrood* comes away from the stick easily, it is ready. Remove and serve.

AND …

You can buy new pieces of wood for your *stokbrood* at most hardware stores. Ask for the wood to be cut into one-metre-long pieces, a safe length that will ensure all braaiers leave with their eyebrows intact. Alternatively just consult the nearest tree regarding some dead branches.

BRAAIED BUTTERNUT SOUP

It's a fact: braaied butternut soup tastes better than ordinary butternut soup. It gets extra flavour when you braai the butternut and onions over the coals. I reckon the main reason all top restaurants don't prepare their butternut soup this way is because they don't have braai facilities in their kitchens.

Once cooked, all you need to transform the contents of the potjie into soup is a potato masher. When you're at home it's easier to use a stick blender though, which also makes the soup smoother.

WHAT YOU NEED (serves 6–8)

1.5 kg butternut
(you might need 2, 3 or 4 butternuts, depending on size)

1 large onion

1 litre chicken stock (or whatever other stock you have on hand)

½ tsp dried thyme
(or 1 tsp fresh chopped thyme)

½ tsp salt

½ tsp black pepper

1 cup cream (250 ml tub)

fresh bread with butter for serving (optional)

WHAT TO DO

1. Peel the butternuts and slice into 2 cm-thick slices. Use a spoon to scrape out the pips and other innards growing in the cavity. Slice the onion in half without peeling it.

2. Braai the butternut and onion on an open or hinged grid over hot coals for about 5–10 minutes. Your aim at this stage is not to cook them completely; you just want the surface a bit charred.

3. When ready, put the braaied butternut and onion in a bowl. Now take off and throw away the outer layer and ends of the onion as you would with any other onion you are about to chop, and then chop the onion.

4. Prepare the stock by boiling the water in your potjie or kettle on the braai or in the kitchen. Add the stock powder or blocks as per the instructions on its packaging. If you're feeling confident, do steps 2 and 4 at the same time.

5. Add the braaied butternut, braaied and chopped onion and thyme to the stock in the potjie and bring to the boil. Put the lid on the pot and cook for 15–30 minutes until the butternut is completely soft and starts to fall apart. You can take the lid off now and again to check that the soup is boiling but not burning, and to check when the butternut is completely soft.

6. Remove the potjie from the fire. Use a regular potato masher (or electric stick blender) and transform the contents of the potjie to soup. Season with salt and pepper.

7. Add the cream and stir well – the texture should be thick but not too solid. If yours is too thick, just add a bit of extra water until you're happy with the consistency.

8. Put the potjie back near the fire to keep the soup hot until you want to serve it.

AND …

You get bonus points if you serve the soup with freshly braaied *roosterkoek* (see page 160).

BABY POTATOES WITH GARLIC, BUTTER AND ROSEMARY

These baby potatoes are right in line with the character of this book – they're very easy to make, yet look impressive and taste great! I boil them first, and then fry them with whole cloves of garlic in butter and rosemary. You squash the potatoes to burst them slightly while they are frying so that the butter and the other flavours can be properly absorbed. It's all done in one pot too, so there's a minimum of dirty dishes.

WHAT YOU NEED
(enough for 6 people as a side dish)

1 kg baby potatoes (washed)

100 g butter, diced
(a fifth of a 500 g brick)

1 tot olive oil

a sprig or 3 of rosemary

all the cloves of one head of garlic (peeled and whole)

1 tsp salt

1 tsp black pepper

WHAT TO DO

1. Cook the potatoes in salted water for about 15 minutes until they are tender (test with a knife or fork).

2. Take the pot off the heat and drain the potatoes. Now put the pot back on the fire and add the butter, olive oil, rosemary, garlic, salt and pepper to the potatoes.

3. Stir until all the butter has melted, and heat further until the butter starts to fry the potatoes. Using a potato masher, the back of a wooden spoon or the bottom of a wine bottle, press down lightly on each potato until they crack open ever so slightly and start to absorb the flavoured butter. Cook for about 10–15 minutes until the potatoes and garlic are golden brown and crispy. You can gently toss or turn the potatoes, but you don't want them to fall apart as we're not making mash here.

4. I like to serve this meal straight from the pot, as the cast iron holds its heat and keeps the potatoes warm until they are on everyone's plates.

AND …

I have a bit of a love–hate relationship with rosemary. It goes very well with some meals, like this one, and you absolutely need to add it. However, in my eating experience some people frequently destroy meals by adding too much rosemary, which then dominates the meal in an unpleasant way. I can only speculate, but think that this is because rosemary is the one herb that grows easily and successfully in most gardens across South Africa. Amateur botanists who fail to nurture most things, find that their rosemary plant flourishes. These people are so proud of the one success story in their herb gardens that they want to show off with it at every opportunity they get, and so go a bit overboard when adding rosemary to food.

CREAMY GARLIC MUSHROOMS (ON TOAST)

I'm a big fan of mushrooms, onions, garlic and cream as individuals. Together they create an exquisite taste, or as Aristotle used to say, 'the whole is greater than the sum of its parts'. It's a nice starter or side dish and is also known to be very popular around the late-night 'atmosfire', as a second braai of the evening.

WHAT YOU NEED
(serves 4–6 as a snack)

2 tots butter

1 tot olive oil

1 onion (chopped)

4 cloves garlic
(crushed or chopped)

500 g whole mushrooms
(brown, button or any mixture of these or others sold commercially for culinary consumption)

1 sprig thyme (stalk removed)

1 tsp salt

½ tsp black pepper

1 cup cream (250 ml tub)

slices of bread
(toasted – optional, to serve)

1 tot finely chopped parsley
(optional, to serve)

WHAT TO DO

1. Heat the oil and butter in a potjie or flameproof pan over a hot fire, add the chopped onion and fry until they become very soft and begin to turn light brown on the edges. Depending on your heat, this will take about 5 minutes.

2. Add the garlic, mushrooms and thyme, then fry until the mushrooms soften and start to brown (your pan needs to be very hot so don't be shy about having a few flames under it). Initially, the mushrooms might struggle to fit into the pan, but they will shrink as they cook.

3. Season with salt and pepper, then pour over the cream and bring to the boil. Simmer the cream for a few minutes, stirring often, until it reduces and forms a thick sauce (it'll darken slightly and turn a shade of grey, like the mushrooms). Timing is pretty important. You need to remove the potjie or pan from the fire when the sauce is thick, but before it has reduced too much and all the sauce is gone. If you don't have time to reduce the whole cup of cream, just use half a cup, but be aware that the meal won't taste quite as awesome.

4. Use a large spoon to scoop the creamy mushrooms onto the toasted bread and serve immediately, topped with finely chopped parsley.

AND ...

The quality of bread used has a direct impact on the end result and your enjoyment of the meal. These days we have a wide variety of great breads available in South Africa and, compared with meat, special breads are relatively cheap so buy the best available. When you walk into an artisan bakery and you feel a bit unsure of yourself, just ask for a sourdough bread. Bunny chow (see page 94) is the exception to the rule; for that, you're supposed (obliged) to use stock-standard white supermarket bread.

When serving braaied food with a slice of bread, you want to butter the bread on one side and toast it over medium coals for the final few minutes of your braai until golden brown. The idea is to have it ready with the rest of the meal.

For any braaied meal in this book that I suggest you serve with bread, you get bonus points if you serve it with freshly braaied *roosterkoek* (see page 160), but I'm not going to mention it on every page, as this would insult your intelligence.

CHEESE FONDUE

There is obviously no need to buy expensive fondue equipment in order to enjoy a traditional cheese fondue. Just make the sauce in one of your smaller cast-iron potjies over the fire. Once the food is ready, move the potjie away from the fire and place a few coals under it to keep the cheese sauce warm and runny, and then tuck in.

WHAT YOU NEED
(serves 4 people as a main meal)

1 block Brie cheese (about 125 g)

1 block Camembert cheese
(about 125 g)

1 block Cheddar cheese
(about 150 g)

1 block Gruyere cheese
(about 150 g)

½ tot cornflour (Maizena)

1 clove garlic (peeled, but whole)

1 cup white wine

1 tot brandy

1 large loaf of bread, cut into bite-sized chunks
(get something nice like a sourdough bread, or at least a baguette)

WHAT TO DO

1. Remove the rinds from all the cheeses. Chop the soft cheeses (Brie and Camembert) into cubes, and grate the hard cheeses. Sprinkle the cornflour over the cheese and toss around. You want the cheese to be thinly dusted with the cornflour.

2. Rub the inside of your small- to medium-sized cast-iron potjie with the piece of garlic.

3. Now put the potjie over coals or a few flames. Pour all of the wine into the pot and bring to a simmer.

4. Add all of the cheese to the simmering wine. Keep stirring while the cheese melts.

5. As soon as you have a smooth sauce, stir in the tot of brandy. Take the potjie off the fire and keep the sauce warm while you enjoy dipping in.

6. Serve with chunks of bread, which everybody can dip into the sauce with suitable implements like sosatie sticks and braai forks.

AND …

You can also dip boiled baby potatoes, cherry tomatoes, mini gherkins or blocks of leftover braaied meat like steak into the sauce.

The traditional Swiss cheese fondue recipes calls for the use of a cherry liqueur known as Kirsch. But this is South Africa and we're preparing the fondue on a fire, so obviously you should rather use brandy. I've had fondue in Switzerland a few times and my South African version tastes better.

SPANAKOPITA

Spanakopita, the classic Greek dish, can be braaied very successfully by using mild coals and a hinged grid. Needless to say, you serve the spanakopita with braaied Greek leg of lamb and Greek salad (see *Fireworks* for both these recipes). Opa!

WHAT YOU NEED (serves 6–10)

1 tot olive oil

1 onion (finely chopped)

600 g spinach
(I prefer baby spinach)

200 g feta (about 3 rounds)

4 eggs (lightly beaten)

1 tsp salt

1 tsp black pepper

2 packets puff pastry
(400 g each; defrosted)

WHAT TO DO

1. Fresh spinach generally contains a fair amount of soil. Rinse thoroughly to get rid of any grittiness, and dry to get rid of excess water. Chop the spinach with your sharpest, newest, most prized knife.

2. Using your biggest pan, fry the onion in the oil until it's soft and starts to turn golden brown. Add the spinach. You may find that you struggle to fit all the spinach in, but as soon as it starts to cook the spinach will wilt down to a fraction of its original size. Let the spinach cook for a few minutes to release any excess moisture, and let that steam off. If you have one, you can also do this step on a stove. The spanakopita will get its braai taste later on anyhow. Take it off the heat and add the fried spinach and onion to a large mixing bowl.

3. Crumble the feta into the mixing bowl, then add the eggs, salt and pepper. Mix well.

4. Unroll the puff pastry and dust each sheet lightly with flour on one side, the side that you'll use on the outside. This will stop the pastry sticking to the grid. If you don't have any flour on hand, you could lightly oil the grid. Put one sheet carefully on the inside of a hinged grid. Spoon the filling evenly over the sheet, leaving a border of about 2 cm empty. Brush this edge with some water. Now put the second sheet on top of the filled bottom layer. Use your hands to press the edges carefully together so that it seals (the water helps the sheets to stick together). Use a knife or fork to prick a few small holes into the pie so that steam can escape while it is cooking.

5. Carefully close the grid, then braai the spanakopita over a medium fire with the grid fairly high for about 20–30 minutes until it is golden brown and cooked. Your only risk is burning the pastry, so rather go too slow than too fast. As you braai, lift the top half of the grid off the surface of the pastry after every time you turn the grid to make sure the pastry doesn't rise or bake 'into' the grid.

6. When it is ready, carefully take the pie off the grid and put it onto a wooden chopping board. Slice into squares or triangles.

UMNGQUSHO (STAMPMIELIES)

Umngqusho is a traditional Xhosa dish made with samp and beans. One of Nelson Mandela's favourites and a perfect side dish to any braaied meat. Samp needs to soak in water overnight, so remember to start the day before.

WHAT YOU NEED (serves 8–10)

500 g samp-and-bean mix

about 4 litres water

1 onion (finely chopped)

2 carrots (chopped)

2 potatoes (peeled and chopped)

1 can chopped tomatoes

125 g onion soup powder (brown or white)

1 tsp salt (optional)

1 cup grated Cheddar cheese

WHAT TO DO

1. Soak the samp and beans overnight in 1 litre of water. The next morning, drain the water off and rinse the samp and beans well.

2. In a large potjie, add the soaked samp and beans and 3 litres of fresh water (no salt). Bring to the boil and cook for 2 hours until almost soft. Control the heat by adding or removing flames and coals so that it's not boiling rapidly but you've got slightly more heat than the very gentle simmer of oxtail potjie. Let's call it a medium-paced simmer. If at any stage it looks like it's too dry in there, add a little more water.

3. Throw in the onion, carrots, potatoes and chopped tomatoes, then simmer for another 30 minutes or until the potatoes are soft. The water level inside the potjie should be just about visible from the top between the samp and beans.

4. The onion soup powder goes in next and you need to stir it in gently until it is well mixed. Continue to simmer uncovered for another 5–15 minutes until most of the moisture has evaporated and you have a thick hearty mixture.

5. Taste the *umngqusho* – if you like it more salty, add a bit of salt. Some onion soup powders are very salty already, so taste first.

6. Take it off the fire and stir in the cheese. Let it stand for 5 minutes, then serve.

AND …

Don't underestimate this meal as it's really good. Serve it as the side dish when you're taking part in the potjiekos competition at your local sports club – it'll put you in a whole different league from all the other guys serving rice.

TAILOR-MADE BRAAI SALT

At some stage during your ascendancy to the braai throne in your backyard, you will want to start mixing your own tailor-made braai salt. This might happen on one of those days when Bafana, the Springboks and the Proteas play on the same day and you are tired of eating meat flavoured with the same commercially bought spice for the seventh time; or it might happen right now, as you read this book.

Use the recipe and ingredients listed below as a broad guideline rather than as an exact list. View it as a point of departure on your journey. Play around with the quantities, leave something out, add something else. To state the blatantly obvious, if you add more of something, the mixture will have a stronger taste of that, and if you add less, it will taste less of that. Normal supermarkets sell all of these spices in ground format, which makes mixing them easier but if you can't find something, go to a speciality spice shop.

WHAT YOU NEED

(makes almost ½ cup of braai spice)

1 tot salt (I like to use high-quality salt flakes and then crush them.)

½ tot ground black pepper

½ tot paprika

½ tot crushed garlic powder

½ tot ground coriander

1 tsp cayenne pepper
(or chilli powder)

1 tsp ground cumin

1 tsp ground cloves

1 tsp ground nutmeg

1 tsp ground allspice (pimento)

WHAT TO DO

1. If some of the ingredients are too big or coarse, solve the problem by taking them for a spin in your coffee grinder or give them some love in your pestle and mortar.

2. Put all the ingredients in a glass jar, then close the lid and shake it well. Use as needed to season steak, chops or chicken. The salt mix also works very well as a dry rub on large meat cuts like beef brisket or pork belly.

3. Over time you might develop more than one mixture for different meats. For chicken you might want to drop the cloves and the nutmeg and add an item like parsley. Perhaps your pork spice will also have some mustard powder in it, for example. But then you would have to kick out one of the other ingredients, as there are already ten, which is a nice round number. Who wants his own tailor-made braai salt with eleven ingredients?

AND ...

The creative process does not stop at choosing the ingredients. You might also want to spend some time or money on choosing a nice glass container or stainless steel shaker to keep your tailor-made braai salt in.

CANNELLONI

This is an Italian classic that I've adapted over time to fit local braai conditions. Although the dish has a number of components, the comforting aspect is that you can make all of it ahead of time and just put the (almost, but not quite) finished product on the fire about 30 minutes before you want to serve the meal. This means you can arrive last at a potjiekos competition, yet finish first (both in terms of time and result). At home, you can also outsource part of the production schedule, for example the baking of the pancakes and the cooking of the bolognese sauce.

WHAT YOU NEED (serves 4–6)

4 cups (1 litre) **pomodoro sauce** (special tomato sauce available in most supermarkets, hidden away in the aisle where all other non-perishable formats of tomatoes are sold; often close to the pasta noodles)

all the ingredients for 1 batch bolognese sauce (see page 20, but leave out the optional cream)

all the ingredients for 1 batch pancakes (see page 194)

½ cup cream

salt and freshly ground black pepper

1 cup grated mozzarella cheese (about 100 g)

½ cup grated Parmesan cheese (about 50 g)

WHAT TO DO

1. Pour 1 cup of pomodoro sauce into the bottom of your large flat-bottomed potjie, and spread it out evenly. You are going to make alternating layers of pomodoro sauce and pancakes.

2. Start filling your pancakes. Throw about 2–3 tots of bolognese sauce on each pancake, then roll it up. Put the rolled pancakes inside the pot, close together. If they don't fit in on the sides, cut some in half. They should lie there like sardines in a tin. Pour another cup of pomodoro sauce over the pancakes, and then continue with another layer until all the pancakes and filling are used up. The number of layers will depend on the diameter of your potjie. Leave space for the cheese on top – the lid shouldn't touch the top of the food.

3. Cover the top layer of the cannelloni with some pomodoro sauce, then pour the cream all over it and season with salt and pepper. Sprinkle over the mozzarella and Parmesan cheese.

4. Put the potjie over a layer of medium-hot coals, and also pack enough hot coals on top of the lid so that the top layer of the cannelloni can bake. Cook for about 30–40 minutes, until the cannelloni is hot and bubbly and the cheese has melted and turned a golden brown colour.

COLESLAW WITH VINEGAR

Vinegar-based coleslaw is the classic side dish to braaied pork. So you, as a complete braaier, need to know this recipe. I prefer to use a mixture of red and green cabbage for a bit of colour on the plate.

WHAT YOU NEED
(serves 6 as a side dish)

3 tots red wine vinegar

1 tot sugar

1 tsp salt

½ tsp black pepper

1 tsp mustard

1 small red cabbage
(washed and finely sliced)

1 small green cabbage
(washed and finely sliced)

4–6 spring onions (chopped)

WHAT TO DO

1. In a small mixing bowl, make the dressing by whisking together the vinegar, sugar, salt, pepper and mustard. You could also shake the ingredients together in a clean glass bottle with a lid.

2. Put the sliced cabbages and spring onions in a large salad bowl. Pour the dressing all over the salad and toss to coat it well. Serve as a side dish to braaied pork.

COLESLAW WITH CARROT AND MAYO

This is a classic braai side dish and making it should be part of your skill set. It is extremely versatile – delicious with braaied chicken and great on pork neck steak burgers. It even complements the spicy taste of boerewors, so add some to your next boerewors roll and transform it into a deluxe version you could impress anyone with.

WHAT YOU NEED
(serves 6 as a side dish)

1 medium head of cabbage
(green or red, finely sliced)

2 large carrots
(peeled and grated)

1 cup mayonnaise or 'salad cream'

1 tot lemon juice

1 tot sugar

1 tsp Dijon mustard

some salt and black pepper
(for seasoning)

WHAT TO DO

1. In a large mixing bowl, toss all of the ingredients together and mix well. That's it!

2. Cover the bowl and refrigerate until ready to serve. The salad can be made a day in advance, as the flavour actually improves overnight.

AND ...

If you feel that was too easy, you can add some raisins and chopped pecan nuts to the mix.

SPICY POTATO SOUP WITH CHORIZO

Considering that it's not meat, you find potatoes at braais quite often. If you add Spanish chorizo chunks (or smoked bacon if you can't find chorizo), here is another great role for the potato at the braai, this time as a soup. The soup is prepared in a potjie that you can position to the side of your main fire and which can be heated by some coals or small pieces of burning wood. This allows you to prepare and enjoy the soup as a starter while you wait for the fire to burn out and form coals for your braai.

WHAT YOU NEED

(serves 6–8 as a starter)

1 piece of chorizo
(about 200 g, or use smoked bacon)

1 packet/bunch of leeks, washed and finely sliced
(about 300 g)

6 large potatoes, peeled and cut into chunks (Yes, in this case you have to peel the potatoes. No, I don't like peeling potatoes either.)

4 cups chicken or vegetable stock

1 cup cream (250 ml tub)

½ cup grated Parmesan cheese (50 g)

1–2 tsp salt

1 tsp black pepper

WHAT TO DO

1. Remove the casing of the chorizo, then slice the meat into small chunks and fry in your cast-iron potjie over hot coals or gentle flames. They are ready when nicely brown but not too dark. Take the chunks out of the pot to use as a garnish later. Leave all the oil that was released by the meat in the pot, as you will use it in the next step.

2. Add the leeks to the pot and fry till soft. This process is similar to frying onions.

3. Now add the potato chunks and stock, and bring to the boil. Cook for about 30–40 minutes until the potato is completely soft and starts to fall apart. You can either put the lid half on the pot or leave the pot completely open.

4. Take the pot off the fire, and use a stick blender to purée it to a smooth, thick consistency. If you don't have a stick blender use a potato masher. Your soup will be less smooth, but will taste about the same. Stir in the cream, Parmesan cheese, salt and pepper, and mix well.

5. Put the pot back on the fire and heat (without boiling) until ready to serve.

6. Garnish each mug or bowl of soup with a few chunks of fried chorizo.

AND ...

Don't be fooled by the simplicity of the ingredients or steps in this recipe. I anticipate that it will rank among the favourites for many of you once you taste it.

ROOSTERKOEK

This is the only recipe from my first book, *Fireworks,* that I have repeated in this book. This is because *roosterkoek* rules at a braai and there are many recipes here that could benefit from adding *roosterkoek* to them. Serve soups and potjie meals with *roosterkoek*, and use *roosterkoek* instead of rolls for any of the burger recipes. Essentially, every time a bread is mentioned for serving with some braaied meal in this book, you'll get bonus points if you bake your own *roosterkoek* instead, even if I don't mention it in that recipe or show it on the photo.

WHAT YOU NEED

(makes 12 decent-sized *roosterkoek*)

1 kg cake flour (as the 'koek' part of the Afrikaans name implies, use cake flour – but white bread flour is also fine if that is what's on hand)

10 g instant yeast
(it comes in 10 g packets)

1 tot sugar

½ tot salt

lukewarm water in a jug
(you'll need roughly just more than 2 cups of water)

2 tots olive oil

WHAT TO DO

1. Sift the flour into a bowl that is at least 3 times as big as 1 kg of flour, and preferably even bigger. If you're in the middle of the bush and don't have a sieve on hand, then skip the sifting part and just chuck the flour into a big enough bowl. If you only have a 1 kg bag of flour and no more, save a little for step 9.

2. Add the yeast and sugar to the flour and mix thoroughly with your clean hand. Now it's time to add the salt and toss the mixture around some more.

3. Pour in the lukewarm water bit by bit and keep kneading the dough. As soon as there is no dry flour left, you've added enough water. Take care not to add too much water, as this will lead to the dough being runny and falling through the grid. *Roosterkoek* falling through the grid is just no good. For 1 kg of flour you'll probably use just a tiny bit more than 2 cups of water.

4. If you think you have enough water in there, add the 2 tots of olive oil.

5. Knead the dough well for about 10 minutes until none of it sticks to your fingers anymore and it forms one big pliable piece.

6. Cover the bowl with a kitchen towel and put in a warm area for 10 minutes.

7. Take off the kitchen towel and knead the dough again for 1 or 2 minutes.

8. Replace the kitchen towel and let it rise for at least 30 minutes.

9. Use your recently washed hands to flatten the dough onto a table or plank that is covered in flour and also lightly sprinkle flour on top of the dough. Your aim is to create a rectangular or square piece of dough.

10. Use a sharp knife and cut the dough into squares, and let them rise for a few minutes one final time.

11. Bake over very gentle coals for about 15–20 minutes, turning often. A *roosterkoek* is ready when it sounds hollow when you tap on it. Alternatively, insert the blade of your pocketknife or multi-tool into them as a test. If the blade comes out clean the *roosterkoek* is ready.

AND ...

Some supermarkets sell fresh dough. If you've bought some of that, start making your *roosterkoek* from step 9.

If you've never made dough in your life, there's no shame in asking someone who has done it before to show you what it means to 'knead it into one pliable piece'.

MACARONI AND CHEESE POTJIE

People refer to certain meals as 'comfort food', which is strange because I find eating most foods comforting. Nonetheless, some foods are more comforting than others, with a macaroni and cheese potjie right up there. You can either serve this as a main course, or as a very impressive side dish to braaied meat like steak, lamb or chicken. If you're serving it as a side to meat, add a crisp green salad to complete the meal.

WHAT YOU NEED (serves 8 as a side dish or 4 as a main course)

500 g macaroni pasta

water and salt (to boil the pasta)

a bit of olive oil

2 tots butter

2 tots cake flour

1 litre milk (4 cups)

400 g mature Cheddar cheese (grated)

1 heaped tsp Dijon mustard

1 tsp salt

1 tsp black pepper

a little bit of ground nutmeg (optional)

WHAT TO DO

1. In a big enough potjie over a hot fire, bring 5 litres of water with about half a tot of salt to boiling point. Add all of the macaroni to the bubbling water and cook for exactly 7 minutes. The noodles will still be slightly undercooked, but they will continue cooking later when baking in the sauce. Drain off all water immediately and drizzle with a little bit of olive oil to prevent the macaroni from sticking together.

2. Return the empty potjie to the fire (not too hot), then add butter and wait until it melts. Add the flour and stir for about 1 minute.

3. Now add the milk bit by bit, stirring continuously. You will notice how the butter and flour mixture first grows and absorbs all the milk you add, and how this thick paste then starts turning into a sauce as you add more and more milk. If you add the milk too quickly, lumps will form. If at any time you notice lumps forming, first stir them vigorously into the rest of the mixture before adding more milk.

4. When all the milk is in, bring the sauce to a slow simmer and add the cheese, mustard, salt and pepper (and nutmeg), and stir well.

5. Now add the cooked macaroni to the sauce, stir to coat the pasta well, then remove the potjie from the fire and cover with a lid until serving time. As the pot will keep its heat for a few minutes, you will be able to quickly braai some steak over very hot coals in this time. Just before serving the pasta, give it another quick toss.

6. If you have cheese left over, sprinkle the grated cheese on top of the meal in the potjie, close the lid and let the cheese melt by placing some coals on top of the lid.

AND ...

For bonus points, you can braai strips of bacon on a grid over the coals (yes, this is possible) or in a pan. Chop them up when they are nice and crispy and mix into the potjie with the pasta during step 5.

The quality and taste of the cheese used will influence the end product. For a recipe like this, I would suggest using Cheddar that was aged for at least 3 months. Using more mature Cheddar or even a variety of mature cheeses like Cheddar, Parmesan, Pecorino, Gruyere and blue cheese will increase the depth of flavour.

SWEET BUTTERNUT AND CREAMED SPINACH

At a steakhouse, they serve two classic side dishes with steak: sweet butternut and creamed spinach. It stands to reason, then, that the discerning braaier needs to know how to prepare them so you can enjoy them with your braaied steak at home. Both are quite easy to make and you can prepare the dishes in advance before your guests arrive. All you have to do then is to reheat the potjies before serving up.

WHAT YOU NEED (serves 6)

For sweet butternut:

1 kg butternut
(peeled and cubed)

½ cup butter

1 tsp salt

½ tsp black pepper

½ tsp ground cinnamon

½ cup brown sugar

2 tots sherry (or orange juice)

For creamed spinach:

800 g fresh spinach
(if you're feeling fancy, buy baby spinach; if you're feeling normal, buy adult spinach)

1 tot olive oil

1 tsp salt

½ tsp black pepper

2 cups cream (2 × 250 ml tubs)

½ tot cornflour
(Maizena mixed with ½ tot water)

½ cup grated mature Cheddar cheese
(if you're still feeling fancy, use something like Parmesan cheese)

WHAT TO DO

Make the butternut:

1. Peel the butternut, cut it open and scrape the seeds and stringy bits out with a spoon. Slice into bite-size cubes.

2. Melt the butter in a flat-bottomed potjie over low coals. Toss in the butternut cubes, salt, pepper, cinnamon, brown sugar and sherry. Stir gently to mix, then bring to a slow simmer.

3. Cover with a lid and cook over low heat for about 30 minutes. Don't take the lid off except for the two brief periods, after 10 and 20 minutes, when you need to stir it. Don't add more water, as the liquid should reduce to a syrup and turn brown on the bottom, and the butternut also releases liquid.

If the dish burns, you had too much heat under the pot, so use less heat next time. If the butternut is still raw after 30 minutes, the opposite is true.

Make the spinach:

1. Wash the spinach well under cold water and then drain off the excess water. Some of the best ways to dry wet spinach are to use a salad spinner, a colander or to pat it dry with a clean kitchen towel. Your wife's hairdryer is not a good idea and that's why it's not on the list.

2. Chop the spinach and specifically pay attention to the thicker stems, making sure they are finely chopped. It goes without saying that this is a great opportunity to practise your chopping skills with your new sharp chef's knife.

3. Heat the oil in a pot and then add the chopped spinach. Fry for a minute, then cover the pot and let it steam to wilt the leaves. Not adding any water means you save the effort of adding water. You don't have to drain off any water at a later stage, and all the flavour stays in the pot. A win, win, win situation so to speak.

4. (Optional step: If you've always wondered when to use the ground nutmeg in your spice rack, now is the time. Add a very small pinch of it to the spinach while you fry it in step 3 for added flavour. It's not worthwhile buying a whole new container of nutmeg just for this recipe, so that's why I left it off the ingredients list, but if you already have it in your kitchen use it now.)

5. Take the lid off after about 5–7 minutes and stir again. The spinach should be wilted by now, but not completely cooked. Add the salt, pepper and cream, then bring to the boil and cook for about 5–8 minutes.

6. Add the cornflour mixture and grated cheese, and then stir while watching it thicken – this will happen quite quickly. Remove from the heat as soon as the mixture is thick. Cover with a lid and set aside until the rest of your meal is ready.

RÖSTI

Pan-fried potato cakes were created by the Swiss as part of their breakfast, where the dish is referred to as a 'rösti'. They are popular all over the world and the Americans call them 'hash browns'. Put simply, they are made from grated potatoes, and are pan-fried until golden brown and crunchy. This is not a main meal but rather a side dish to something else that you're going to braai, say for example a steak.

WHAT YOU NEED (makes 2 large pan-size röstis; serves 4)

1 onion (peeled)

4 medium potatoes
(if you like peeling potatoes, peel them; but if you're similar to me and don't like peeling potatoes, don't)

1 tsp salt

½ tsp pepper

1 tot olive oil

1 tot butter

WHAT TO DO

1. Grate the onion and potatoes with the coarse side of your grater and toss them into a mixing bowl. Add the salt and pepper and mix well.

2. In a flat-bottomed cast-iron pot or flameproof pan over a medium-hot fire, heat the oil and butter together. Then put the rösti mixture into the pan, using an egg lifter or a spatula to flatten each rösti by putting some pressure on it. You can either make one big rösti at a time that fills the whole pan, or make a few smaller röstis together in the pan. The latter option is easier, as one big rösti sometimes breaks when you turn it. Whichever route you go, the rösti should be about 1 cm thick. Fry until golden brown on both sides, which should take about 3–5 minutes a side over medium heat.

3. Remove from the pan. If you made smaller röstis, they can be served whole, and if you made bigger röstis you can slice them into quarters.

COUSCOUS

Basic couscous is incredibly easy to make, and from there on your possibilities are endless. Couscous doesn't need any cooking and you literally just add water to it. Once prepared, basic couscous should be seen as a blank canvas ready for you to create a masterpiece with. Play around by adding different combinations of herbs, spices, vegetables, meats, nuts and cheeses.

WHAT YOU NEED (serves 6)

3 cups uncooked couscous (about 500 g)

water

1 tsp salt

½ tsp black pepper

2 tots of olive oil or butter

Additions to make a couscous masterpiece:

Option 1: Mediterranean style

1 cup pitted olives

2 rounds feta cheese (about 150 g, cubed)

2 cups cherry tomatoes (sliced in half)

1 tot basil (chopped)

2 tots extra-virgin olive oil

Option 2: Bosveld style

1 cup sliced biltong (if the slices are really big, slice them into smaller chunks)

1 cup roasted cashew nuts, peanuts or a mix of the two

1–2 tsp of your tailor-made braai salt (see page 152)

1 tot parsley (chopped)

Option 3: Moroccan style

2 small red chillies (chopped)

1 tot pine nuts (toasted)

2 rounds feta cheese (about 150 g, cubed)

1 can of chickpeas (drained)

2 tsp paprika

1 tot fresh mint (chopped)

WHAT TO DO

1. Boil at least 1 litre of water in a kettle or pot. Don't look at the kettle while you're waiting, as a watched kettle never boils.

2. While you are waiting for the water to boil, throw all the couscous into a mixing bowl. Use a bowl made from glass, ceramic, stainless steel, enamel or anything else that will be happy with the boiling water you are about to pour into it. Add the salt and pepper to the uncooked couscous and give it a good stir. Do not use your wife's fancy new salad bowl made from very thin glass as it might break. You can transfer the couscous salad to that bowl afterwards for serving it, but you can't prepare it in that bowl.

3. Pour boiling water into the couscous until all the couscous is covered with water. As soon as all the couscous is covered, and there is an ever-so-thin layer of water on top of the couscous, you have enough water in there. Cover the bowl with a lid, plate, tray, cutting board, cling wrap or any other suitable object and let it stand for 6 minutes.

4. After 6 minutes, take the cover off and use a fork to 'fluff' up the couscous. Stir in your choice of olive oil or butter. The couscous is now ready to eat. It can be used just like this as a side dish to potjie as a substitute for rice to soak up the sauce. Alternatively, you can turn it into a couscous masterpiece by adding the ingredients given in Option 1, 2 or 3.

VODKA PASTA

There used to be an Italian bistro in Stellenbosch that served a delicious meal called 'vodka pasta'. Back in the early days of National Braai Day, when I was still fresh out of my corporate job and the canteen that went with it, I often visited this bistro and had the 'vodka pasta' for lunch. Unfortunately the bistro has closed since then (and fortunately National Braai Day has grown!), so these days I just make my version of the pasta in a potjie over a fire.

WHAT YOU NEED (serves 4–6)

500 g pasta (for this meal I prefer penne, but use what you like)

1 tot olive oil

1 tot butter

1 onion (very finely chopped)

1 pack bacon (sliced or diced)

2 cloves garlic (finely chopped)

2 cans whole tomatoes, puréed (or 2 cans chopped tomatoes)

½ tot sugar

1 tsp salt

½ tsp pepper

1 cup cream (250 ml tub)

½ cup vodka

Parmesan cheese (to serve)

WHAT TO DO

1. In your potjie on a fire, cook the pasta in salted water for 6 minutes, then drain it and keep it on one side. The pasta won't be completely cooked but this is what you want, as it will be finished later.

2. Put the same (now empty) potjie back on the fire, heat the oil and butter, then fry the bacon and onion until the onion is soft but not too brown. It will take between 5 and 10 minutes. Add the garlic and then fry for another minute.

3. Now add the chopped tomatoes, sugar, salt and pepper. Stir well, then cover and simmer for 15 minutes until it gets thicker.

4. Add the cream, then stir well and bring it to the boil. As soon as it is boiling, add the half-cooked pasta from step 1 and pour in the vodka. Bring it to the boil again, then cook for about 5 minutes until the sauce thickens and the pasta starts to absorb the sauce.

5. Remove from the fire and serve. As with any tomato-based pasta, you can serve it with grated or shaved Parmesan cheese, and as with almost any pasta, tomato base or not, you can drizzle it with quality South African extra-virgin olive oil.

6. Serve with salt and pepper on the table, so guests can add their own.

MINESTRONE

The word 'minestrone' literally means 'Italian vegetable soup', which is exactly what it is. Unlike the butternut and potato soup in this book, which should be served smooth and thick, you leave minestrone in its natural chunky form. This means that the preparation is incredibly simple. You just have to put your potjie over a fire and then add the ingredients as described in each step. Every region (and almost every household) in Italy has its own version, and there is no standard recipe for minestrone. There is no definitive ingredient either, but the inclusion of cannellini beans is very traditional and that's why I use them in my recipe. If you've never had the confidence to make potjiekos before, start off with this recipe.

WHAT YOU NEED (serves 6–8)

2 tots olive oil

1 packet bacon
(200–250 g, finely chopped)

1 onion (finely chopped)

2 garlic cloves (finely chopped)

2 celery stalks (finely chopped)

2 carrots
(peeled and finely chopped)

6 cups water (1.5 litres)

2 cups chicken or vegetable stock (or whatever stock you have at home)

1 can cannellini beans (or other white beans; drained and rinsed)

2 cans chopped tomatoes

1 cup uncooked pasta
(small shapes)

1 cup shelled peas
(I use frozen peas)

salt and pepper (to taste)

grated Parmesan cheese
(to serve)

fresh bread (optional, to serve)

WHAT TO DO

1. In a large potjie (no. 3) over a medium-hot fire, heat the oil and then throw in the bacon, onion, garlic, celery and carrots. Fry for about 10 minutes until the vegetables start to soften and the bacon starts to brown.

2. Add the water, stock, beans and tomatoes to the pot. Cover with a lid and bring to a simmer. Cook for 15 minutes.

3. Take off the lid and add the pasta. Simmer for a further 10 minutes or until the pasta is soft but not soggy.

4. Add the peas and stir well. The frozen peas will be ready to eat by the time you dish up. Taste the soup and season with salt and pepper according to your own taste. The bacon and stock already contain salt, so it's possible that the soup may not need extra salt.

5. Serve in deep bowls with grated Parmesan cheese and bread.

MIELIEPAPTERT

In a world of uncertainty, I have never been disappointed by *mieliepaptert*. It's an almost foolproof dish. You start off by making *mieliepap*, already a great meal on its own. Then you just add some bells and whistles to make it even better – almost like buying a great new car and then adding all the optional extras. Assembling the *mieliepaptert* in layers is essentially like making a lasagne, just with entirely different ingredients.

WHAT YOU NEED (serves 8)

For the *stywepap*:

3 cups water

1 tsp salt

2 cups maize meal

For the *mieliepaptert*:

2 tots olive oil

1 onion (finely chopped)

1 packet (200–250 g) **smoked streaky bacon** (sliced into chunks)

400–500 g mushrooms (sliced)

½ tsp salt
(the bacon is already salty)

½ tsp black pepper

1 can creamed sweet corn

2 cups grated Cheddar cheese
(about 200 g)

2 cups cream (2 × 250 ml tubs)

2 sprigs fresh thyme

WHAT TO DO

Make the *stywepap*:

1. Add the water and the salt to a pot and get the water boiling over a hot fire (or stove).

2. When the water in the pot boils, stir in the maize meal using a wooden spoon. It should take you between 1 and 2 minutes to mix it in properly.

3. Put the lid on the pot and let it simmer for 25 minutes on very low heat. On a fire, this means removing the pot from the flames and placing it on a few coals.

4. You can check on the porridge (or *pap*) once or twice during this time to make sure it's simmering (boiling is too hot; standing still is too cold), but don't lift the lid too often as too much water will then escape in the form of steam. After 25 minutes the porridge will be ready.

5. You can now enjoy the porridge as is, but to use it in *mieliepaptert* you need to take it off the fire and let it cool down in the pot – we're looking for a solid piece of pap that we can slice.

Make the *mieliepaptert*:

1. Take the cooled *stywepap* out of the pot in one piece, and cut into 1 cm-thick slices, as you would do with bread.

2. Put the pot back on the fire. Add the oil, onion, bacon and mushrooms. Fry for about 10 minutes until the onion turns a golden brown colour. Season with salt and pepper.

3. Take the pot off the heat and pour the contents into a bowl. In the empty pot, start layering the *paptert* with a layer of sliced *pap* (place a few slices of *pap* loosely next to each other, but not too tightly). Follow with a layer of onion/bacon/mushrooms, a few spoonfuls of sweet corn and some grated Cheddar. Then another layer of *pap*, and so on. You should have about 2–3 layers (but this is not an exact science) of each, finishing with some cheese.

4. Pour the cream over the top layer (it will sink in), and finish with some thyme leaves.

5. Put the lid back on. Put the pot over some coals (not too hot) and also put some hot coals on top of the lid. Cook for 30 minutes until the meal is simmering and the cheese is nice and brown. The cream sauce will thicken on standing, so leave it to rest for 10–15 minutes before serving.

MEDITERRANEAN-STYLE STUFFED FLATBREAD

Here you will meet the fancy cousin of *roosterkoek*, the one who goes for skiing holidays in Europe. Don't be scared of working with dough – with a bit of practice you'll soon get the hang of it. As with quite a few other braaied meals, literally the only challenge in perfecting this is not to burn it.

WHAT YOU NEED (serves 6–8 as a side dish or starter)

4 cups white bread flour

1 sachet instant yeast (10 g)

2 tsp sugar

1 tsp salt

1½ cups lukewarm water

1 tot extra-virgin olive oil (plus a little extra for greasing the dough)

about 20 black olives (pitted and halved)

2 rounds of feta cheese (about 150 g)

1 tot rosemary (finely chopped)

4 sundried tomatoes (the soft ones, preserved in oil, roughly chopped)

some water (for brushing)

good-quality South African olive oil (for dipping the bread into to eat)

WHAT TO DO

1. In a large bowl, mix the flour, yeast, sugar and salt together.

2. Add the water and olive oil and mix with your clean hands until a sticky dough forms. Now knead this until the dough becomes soft and elastic, and is in the shape of a ball.

3. Drizzle a bit of olive oil onto the dough and lift it out of the bowl. Use your hands to spread the olive oil in a thin coat all over it. Put it back in the bowl, cover with plastic wrap and let it rise in a warm area for about 30 minutes until doubled in size.

4. On a well-floured surface, roll out the dough into an oval shape of about 30–40 cm long. Brush the surface lightly with some water. Basically, you just need the top side of the rolled-out dough to be damp.

5. Spread the olives, feta, rosemary and sundried tomato chunks on one half of the dough, then fold the uncovered area over onto the toppings. Pinch the sides together to close them (the water in step 4 will help the two sides to stick together). Your flatbread will be about 20 cm long if you folded it right.

6. Sprinkle the top with a little flour, then flatten the whole thing slightly by pressing down on all parts of the folded dough with your hands.

7. Transfer the dough carefully and quickly onto the one half of a hinged braai grid and then close the grid. You could ask your braai assistant to help you with this.

8. Your biggest risk when braaing bread like this one is that it will burn. Braai over medium coals, with the grid set fairly high just like you would braai *roosterkoek*. Turn the bread often but gently. The bread is ready when it makes a hollow sound when you tap it, which should take around 20–25 minutes. During the braai it's also a good idea to loosen and lift the top half of the grid after every time you turn it. This will lessen the chances that your bread will be stuck in the grid at the end of the braai.

When ready, remove from the fire and grid and let cool for 5–10 minutes on a wooden board. Slice and enjoy as is, or dipped in olive oil.

SPANISH OMELETTE

The first time I ate a Spanish omelette was a few years ago on the island of Majorca. The restaurant was right on the beach and for that Spanish omelette and me, it was love at first bite. What sets this omelette apart from its normal omelette competitors is the potato. This is a great meal to prepare for a breakfast braai, and the perfect way to start a day.

WHAT YOU NEED (serves 4)

500–600 g potatoes
(about 2 large potatoes)

2 tots olive oil

1 small onion (finely sliced)

1 tsp salt

½ tsp black pepper

6 eggs (beaten)

WHAT TO DO

1. Put the potatoes in a small pot. Add some water to just cover the top of the potatoes and then bring to the boil. Boil for about 25 minutes until they are just cooked, but not too soft.

2. Take the potatoes out of the pot and slice them into fairly thin slices. I like to keep the skins on, but you're welcome to remove them at this stage.

3. In a medium-sized pan, heat the oil, then add the onion and fry for 5 minutes over medium heat until it starts to brown.

4. Slide the potatoes into the pan, then continue to fry until the potatoes are tender and start to colour (don't brown them). Take care when you flip the potato slices and don't break them apart too much.

5. Add the salt and pepper to the beaten eggs, then pour the eggs into the pan – it will run into all the corners between the potatoes and the onions, so no need to stir it. Fry for 5–10 minutes over medium-low heat (not too hot) until the top is almost set but still soft. Carefully put a plate on top of the pan, then flip it around and slide the omelette back into the pan – the fried side will now be facing up. Tip any runny egg left in the plate back into the side of the pan.

6. Fry for another 1 or 2 minutes until the omelette is cooked. At this stage, there is nothing stopping you from distributing a bit of grated cheese over the top of the meal.

7. Take it out of the pan and serve it hot or cold.

AND ...

This is a great way to use up leftover boiled potatoes from the braai the night before. If there happen to be some leftover green peas from the night before, add them to the mix as well.

VEGETABLE POCKETS

Root vegetables like carrots and beetroot are great on the fire – in fact when you prepare them like this they are actually entirely edible. The heat from the fire caramelises the natural sugars in the vegetables and you're left with all sorts of wonderful flavours in this side dish.

WHAT YOU NEED
(for 6 side portions)

2 cups beetroot chunks
(about 2 cm × 2 cm)

2 cups carrot chunks

2 cups onion wedges

12–18 whole garlic cloves
(smaller is better in this case)

3 sprigs fresh thyme (stalks off)

rind and juice of half a lemon
(rind finely grated)

1 tsp salt

½ tsp black pepper

3 tots olive oil
(roughly ½ tot per pocket)

You'll also need:

6 squares of foil
(about 30 cm × 30 cm each)

WHAT TO DO

1. Put the beetroot, carrots, onion, garlic, thyme leaves, lemon rind, lemon juice, salt, pepper and oil in a large bowl. Toss to mix well.

2. Divide into 6 portions and put each portion in the middle of a square of foil (shiny side up). Make sure that each helping has roughly the same amount of oil and vegetables.

3. Bring the ends of the foil together to create a loose pocket, then squeeze the top together to seal it. We want them to roast and steam at the same time.

4. Put the pockets over relatively high heat on a low grid (not directly on the coals), then cook them for about 30 minutes (the exact time will depend on the heat). Take one of the pockets off the heat, open it and test with a sharp knife to see if the vegetables are cooked. They should have a nice brown colour on the bottom and be tender.

HOW TO COOK RICE

As you can serve many meals in this book with rice, I thought it a good idea to include a proper description on how you should prepare it. There are no secrets; it's just a question of adding enough water and not overcooking it. Not all types of rice cook for the same length of time. Whichever type you prefer, one cup of uncooked rice will serve 4–6 people once cooked.

NORMAL RICE (LONG GRAIN/PARBOILED)

WHAT YOU NEED

6 cups water

½ tot salt

1 cup rice

WHAT TO DO

1. In a large pot on the fire or stove, bring the water and salt to the boil.

2. When boiling, add the rice and cook for 20–25 minutes.

3. Drain the rice in a colander, and quickly rinse with very hot water. Let it stand for 5 minutes before serving.

BASMATI RICE

WHAT YOU NEED

6 cups water

½ tot salt

1 cup rice

WHAT TO DO

1. In a large pot on the fire or stove, bring the water and salt to the boil.

2. When boiling, add the rice and cook for 12 minutes.

3. Drain the rice in a colander, and quickly rinse with very hot water. Let it stand for 5–10 minutes before serving. Separate the grains with a fork if necessary.

JASMINE RICE

WHAT YOU NEED

1 cup rice

3 cups water

6 cups water

½ tot salt

WHAT TO DO

1. Put the rice and 3 cups of water in a mixing bowl. Soak for 15 minutes, then drain off the water and rinse the rice under running water.

2. In a large pot on the fire or stove, bring the 6 cups of water and salt to the boil.

3. When boiling, add the soaked and rinsed rice and cook for 15 minutes.

4. Drain the rice in a colander, and quickly rinse with very hot water. Let it stand for 5 minutes before serving.

BROWN AND WILD RICE

WHAT YOU NEED

3 cups water

½ tot salt

1 cup rice

WHAT TO DO

1. In a large pot on the fire or stove, add the water, salt and rice and bring to the boil.

2. Reduce the heat to very low, then cover with a lid and simmer for 35–40 minutes. When all of the water has been absorbed, the rice is cooked and ready. You don't need to strain or rinse it.

DESSERTS

I'M NOT ONE FOR
ADDING SUGAR TO MY
COFFEE AS I LIKE THE
TASTE OF COFFEE. IF
YOU WANT SOMETHING
SWEET, MAKE A
PROPER DESSERT.

BRANDY TIRAMISU

I know this is not a meal you make on a fire but, first, it's one of my favourite desserts. And second, it contains brandy, which not only gives it a nice South African flavour but also makes it a *de facto* braai dish. A word of caution: one of the ingredients is castor sugar and you have to use that; normal sugar simply does not work. I've bumped my head so that you don't have to.

WHAT YOU NEED

(serves 4–6, depending on the size of your serving glasses)

3 eggs (separated)

¾ cup castor sugar

250 g mascarpone cheese (1 tub)

1 cup strong black coffee (chilled)

3 tots brandy

1 box sponge fingers (like Boudoir biscuits)

some cocoa powder (for decoration)

WHAT TO DO

1. Separate the eggs into two mixing bowls, one for yolks and one for whites. This is really not difficult, but if you've never done it before, ask someone for help. A bit of egg white in the yolk bowl is not a crisis, but make sure that there are no bits of yolk with the whites, otherwise the whites won't whip to stiff peaks.

2. Using a clean and dry hand whisk or electric beaters, whisk the egg whites in a mixing bowl until they are thick, hold their shape and form stiff peaks when you lift the whisk out of the egg.

3. Using another mixing bowl, use the same whisk to beat the egg yolks and castor sugar until the mixture turns a pale yellow colour and doubles in volume. Add the mascarpone cheese and whisk until the mixture is smooth.

4. Using a large metal spoon, add half of the whisked egg whites to the mascarpone mixture, folding it in. This means to carefully stir the mixture in a figure-of-eight motion without losing any of the airiness and volume that we created while whisking. When the mixture is smooth, add the remaining half of the egg whites, folding it in again until the mixture is smooth and thick, almost like a mousse. Set it aside.

5. Mix the coffee with the brandy in a large mug so that it's ready for the next step.

6. To assemble: Fill four to six brandy glasses two-thirds of the way with the Tiramisu mixture from step 4. Briefly dip each biscuit into the coffee mixture and then press the biscuits vertically down into the Tiramisu-filled glasses, using about four biscuits per glass. Don't soak the biscuits in the coffee mixture otherwise they will be too soft. If there is any Tiramisu mixture left, fill up the glasses equally with it. The ends of the biscuits will probably show – that's fine. Sift or sprinkle a thin layer of cocoa powder over the top and refrigerate.

AND ...

Make this at least 4–6 hours ahead of your braai, as the biscuits need time to soften and the flavour needs time to develop.

The Tiramisu is even better if you prepare it a day in advance.

You can also make it in one large rectangular dish. Arrange the soaked biscuits in two layers, covering each layer of biscuits with a layer of Tiramisu mixture – almost like assembling lasagne.

BENCHMARK MALVA PUDDING IN A POTJIE

Some time in the late 1970s food guru Michael Olivier, who was responsible for the Boschendal Restaurant, asked his friend Maggie Pepler to come and teach them how to make the original malva pudding. Ever since, it's been a permanent fixture on their buffet menu. My malva pudding recipe is based on that original recipe and is published with Michael's blessing. The single biggest adjustment from the original recipe is that I bake the pudding in a no. 10 flat-bottomed baking potjie on the fire, and not in a conventional oven.

WHAT YOU NEED (serves 6)

For the batter:

1 cup flour

½ tot bicarbonate of soda

1 cup white sugar

1 egg

1 tot apricot jam

1 tot vinegar

1 tot melted butter

1 cup milk

For the sauce:

½ cup cream

½ cup milk

1 cup sugar

½ cup hot water

½ cup butter

WHAT TO DO

1. Light the fire. You need fewer coals than when braaing steak, but you'll need a steady supply of coals once the pudding is baking. Now use butter to grease your no. 10 flat-bottomed baking potjie. You can see a picture of this kind of potjie on page 13.

2. Sift the flour and the bicarbonate of soda into a large bowl and stir in the sugar (you don't need to sift the sugar).

3. In another mixing bowl, whisk the egg very well. Now add the jam, vinegar, butter and milk, whisking well after adding each ingredient.

4. Add the wet ingredients of step 3 to the dry ingredients of step 2 and mix well.

5. Pour the batter into the potjie, put on the lid and bake for 50 minutes by placing some coals underneath the potjie and some coals on top of the lid. Don't add too much heat, as burning is a big danger. There is no particular risk in having too little heat and taking up to 1 hour to get the baking done, so rather go too slow than too fast. During this time, you can add a few fresh hot coals to the bottom and top of the potjie whenever you feel the pudding is losing steam.

6. When the pudding has been baking for about 40 minutes (about 10 minutes before it's done), heat all the sauce ingredients in a small potjie over medium coals. Keep stirring to ensure that the butter is melted and the sugar is completely dissolved, but don't let it boil. If you want a (slightly) less sweet pudding, use half a cup of sugar and a full cup of hot water for the sauce, instead of the other way round as per the ingredients list.

7. After about 50 minutes of baking, insert a skewer into the middle of the pudding to test whether it's done. If the skewer comes out clean, it's ready.

8. Take the pudding off the fire and pour the sauce evenly over it. Believe me, it will absorb all the sauce – you just need to leave it standing for a few minutes. Serve the malva pudding warm with a scoop of vanilla ice-cream, a dollop of fresh cream or a puddle of vanilla custard. A good way to keep it hot is to put it near the fire, but not too close – after doing everything right, we don't want it to burn now.

AND ...

In the original recipe, the tot measures of apricot jam, butter and vinegar as well as the half tot of bicarbonate of soda are all given as 1 tablespoon each. These minor changes won't affect the outcome of the dessert but for the sake of accurately recording history, I think it's important that we note it.

APPLE TART IN A POTJIE

I first learnt to make apple tart with my friend Louis Jonker, the renowned part-time chef from Stellenbosch (at home he and his wife Anita split the cooking half-and-half). Once, during a visit to Ceres in the Western Cape, I decided to try something I'd never seen before (but it has since grown to such fame that it's now standard practice) – apple tart in a potjie! I adjusted the recipe slightly for cooking on a fire, and the end result was very successful. Try it and see for yourself!

WHAT YOU NEED (serves 6–8)

For the filling:

8–10 Granny Smith apples
(Louis and all the Ceres locals assured me that when baking apple tart, Granny Smith apples are the way to go)

½ cup water

½ cup raisins

1 tsp cinnamon

2 tots brandy (or rum)

For the crumble:

1½ cups cake flour

1½ cups brown sugar
(caramel brown sugar, or ordinary light brown sugar)

125 g salted butter
(a quarter of a 500 g block – soft)

another 2 tots butter

another dash of cinnamon

vanilla ice-cream
(or cream, to serve)

WHAT TO DO

1. Peel and core the apples, cut them into chunks and throw them in a potjie. Add the water, raisins, cinnamon and brandy, and mix well.

2. Put the potjie on the fire, with the lid on. Cook the mixture for about 10 minutes until the apples begin to soften. Remove from the fire once cooked.

3. While the apples and their friends cook, add the flour, sugar and butter to a bowl and rub together with your clean fingertips until it forms a dry, crumbly mixture.

4. Add half of the crumble mixture to the potjie and mix it into the cooked apples.

5. Use the rest of the crumble mixture to cover the apples – make sure it spreads out evenly.

6. Add a couple of knobs of butter on top of the crumble and sprinkle a bit of cinnamon over the top to give the tart some colour. Put the lid on the potjie and go back to the fire.

7. Put the potjie over gentle coals and also put coals on the lid. When and if the coals lose power, add extra coals to the bottom and top of the potjie. If the fire is big and one side of the potjie gets more heat than the other, rotate the potjie every now and again. Bake for about 45 minutes to an hour, until you see the apple sauce bubbling through the crust when you lift the lid.

8. Enjoy with some vanilla ice-cream or cream.

SAGO PUDDING

Sago pudding is like my brother and sisters; something that I grew up with and that both my mother and my father love. The starchy white sago grains are made from a paste that comes from the sago palm, which grows in tropical places like the East Indies. But never fear – sago pudding is an authentic South African ending to a proper South African braai. In my family, we served sago with a sprinkling of cinnamon sugar and a bit of apricot jam, which you might or might not consider normal.

WHAT YOU NEED (serves 4–6)

1 litre milk (conveniently, almost every supermarket in the world sells milk in this measurement unit)

1 cup sago

½ cup sugar

2 tots butter

1 cinnamon stick

3 eggs

1 tsp vanilla essence

4 tots apricot jam

cinnamon sugar (see below)

WHAT TO DO

1. Throw the milk and sago into your flat-bottomed potjie and mix. Cover with the lid and let it stand for at least 1 hour – longer is also absolutely fine.

2. After an hour (or longer) add the sugar, butter and cinnamon stick to the sago and milk, then mix everything together. The butter will obviously not mix into the cold ingredients at this stage.

3. Put the potjie on the fire (coals or flames) and bring to a gentle simmer without the lid on. Control the heat (you might need to remove some coals or flames from under the potjie) and simmer gently for about 15 minutes until the grains have swollen up and the sago has become almost see-through. Don't multi-task at this stage, as milk can easily boil over – you have been warned. If you're going to err one side or another, rather simmer it for too long than too short, but please don't let it boil over or burn. Take the potjie off the fire and leave it to cool slightly with or without the lid on for at least 10 minutes (again, longer is acceptable).

4. Whisk the eggs and vanilla until they are well mixed and quite fluffy. Pour the mixture into the sago, stirring all the time.

5. Spoon the apricot jam in blobs on top of the sago mixture in the potjie, and then sprinkle with cinnamon sugar.

6. Put the lid on the potjie and bake for 30 minutes by placing coals underneath the potjie and also placing coals on its lid.

AND ...

To make the cinnamon sugar, just mix 1 teaspoon of ground cinnamon with 2 tots of sugar and stir well.

PANCAKES

When I was small, pancakes were usually something we ate in wintertime, and my mother made them in a pan on the kitchen stove. The other place to find great pancakes was the church bazaar where they were made on gas stoves and almost exclusively served with cinnamon sugar and a squeeze of lemon juice. But all of that changed a few years ago when I became good friends with some Dutch people. They eat pancakes all the time and with various fillings. The most memorable pancake experience with my Dutch friends was on a camping trip in Botswana when they served me breakfast in my tent consisting of pancakes with a cheese-and-bacon filling.

WHAT YOU NEED

(makes 15–20, depending on size of pan)

2 cups cake flour

2 cups water

2 extra-large eggs

1 tsp lemon juice

½ tsp salt

½ tot vegetable oil

more vegetable oil (for frying)

WHAT TO DO

1. Mix all the ingredients together in a large bowl with a hand whisk until the batter is smooth and there are no lumps. For best results, leave the batter to rest for at least 30 minutes before using it.

2. People sometimes say I discriminate against gas braais, but this is not true. Here you go – the one recipe in this book where I believe those single-burner, camping gas stoves work very well for braaing something. On the topic of equipment, there is a reason why men like me can cook pancakes these days, and it's called a non-stick pan – use one.

3. First heat the pan with a little oil in it and then pour enough batter into the pan to cover the whole of the bottom with a thin layer. I find that a soup ladle works best for this. Tip and swivel the pan so that the batter can run to the ends of the pan. Fry for about 2–3 minutes until the pancake comes loose, then use a spatula to turn it over and fry on the other side.

4. Slide the pancake from the pan onto a plate and add the filling of your choice. Depending on the filling, you will either roll the pancake or fold it into a quarter of its original size before serving.

Filling suggestions:

- cinnamon sugar and a squeeze of lemon juice (the obvious one)
- Cheddar cheese and crispy fried bacon
- chocolate or hazelnut spread (like Nutella)
- whipped cream and tinned caramel
- chicken mayonnaise (see page 74)
- bolognese sauce (see page 20) with grated Parmesan cheese

GLÜHWEIN

Glühwein originates in Germany but is also very popular in Austria, which is not surprising as Austria is essentially like a holiday province of Germany if we have to be honest. Glühwein is served in the snow on ski slopes, in mountain huts and at European Christmas markets. Always drink Glühwein hot, and you'll enjoy it best when the temperature around you is very low, for example around a campfire in the Kalahari or Karoo, while you're freezing your backside off.

WHAT YOU NEED (serves 4)

1 bottle red wine

rind of 1 orange
(peeled off with a vegetable peeler)

rind of 1 lemon
(peeled off with a vegetable peeler)

1 cup orange juice

1 cinnamon stick

1 whole star anise

2 cardamom pods

4 cloves

½ cup sugar

WHAT TO DO

1. Mix all the ingredients in an old-school camp kettle or flameproof pot, then put it over a medium-hot fire and bring to a slow simmer.

2. Cover with a lid and simmer over low heat (slowly) for about 15 minutes, stirring occasionally until the sugar has dissolved completely. Let it stand for 15 minutes near the fire (perhaps with a few coals under it) so that the drink can stay hot, but is not boiling too rapidly.

3. Strain through a sieve into mugs and throw away the rind and spices. Always serve hot.

AND ...

In Europe, it is not uncommon to add an extra shot of brandy or rum to each mug of Glühwein when you're really freezing. You might, for example, be really cold if you've spent the whole afternoon hunting Springbok in the glacial conditions of the winter's Karoo veld. Then it's better to wait for the Glühwein until your rifle is packed away though.

ACKNOWLEDGEMENTS

Writing and publishing a book is one of those things that I always wanted to do at some stage of my life (and this does not make me special). For most of my life I just had absolutely no idea what that book might be about. And then through the unique direction my life took with the establishment and growth of National Braai Day, it came to the point that the accumulated knowledge in my head meant that there was a book to be written on how to braai, and then a second book (this one) to explore the topic even further.

Even though you see my face on the cover, producing a book like this alone is a project way beyond my capabilities. And so, after the success of *Fireworks* (my first book) I was in the fortunate position of not only having the opportunity to write another book, but also to assemble a dream-team around me for the project.

- Louise Grantham and Russell Clarke from Bookstorm stand central to the piece of food and life literature that you are holding in your hands.

- Food stylist Brita du Plessis and photographer Matthys van Lill are two individuals right at the top of their respective games. They are the reason why the photos in this book are so phenomenally awesome.

- When I first met Ilse van der Merwe, she told me she reckoned she could help. Turns out she was right. I can confidently say that you can serve the meals from this book with confidence. Ilse has fine-tuned them to perfection.

- My good friend Stephanus Rabie toured with me on many braai adventures over the past few years. He is also a very gifted photographer and is responsible for the pictures on pages 1, 6 and 198.

- For this book we did not use one, but two editors. Pat Botes and Tildie Williams gave their respective inputs, which then fed back into the manuscripts. For the Afrikaans edition I had the additional help of the brilliant Theunis Strydom who sometimes knows what I'm trying to say before I even say it.

- Once the book is at the printers there is a massive support team at Pan Macmillan (on the English side) as well as Human & Rousseau (on the Afrikaans side); their combined efforts have led us to where we are today.

Lastly I would like to thank and applaud every single individual who reads this book. We live in the best country in the world so let's celebrate that on a daily basis around a fire. What better way than to continually push the culinary boundaries and produce excellent meals in this traditional style of cooking! There are 11 official languages in South Africa – in all 11 of those we use the word braai!

Text © Jan Braai
Photographs © Jan Braai

All rights reserved. No part of this book may be reproduced or transmitted in any form or by any means, electronic or mechanical, including photocopying, recording or any information storage or retrieval system, without permission from the copyright holder.

ISBN: 978-1-920434-50-2

First edition, first impression 2013

Published jointly by
Bookstorm (Pty) Limited   Pan Macmillan South Africa
PO Box 4532   Private Bag X19
Northcliff 2115   Northlands 2116
Johannesburg   Johannesburg
South Africa   South Africa
www.bookstorm.co.za   www.panmacmillan.co.za

Distributed by Pan Macmillan
via Booksite Afrika

Edited by Pat Botes
Proofread by John Henderson
Food styled by Brita du Plessis
Photography by Matthys van Lill
Cover design by Jacob LC Erasmus
Book design by Triple M Design
Printed by Ultra Litho (Pty) Ltd, Johannesburg

INDEX

JAN BRAAI SAYS ...

1. If you're in any doubt as to whether your fire is big enough, then your fire is not big enough.

2. Wealthy urban and poor rural people all braai with wood – it's the great equaliser.

3. For my recipes you need three measurement tools: cups, tots and teaspoons. A tot glass is that same little glass they serve shots from in pubs. Even in the middle of nowhere, you should be able to guess with reasonable accuracy the size of a cup, a tot and a teaspoon.

4. If you think the meat is ready to come off the fire, then take it off. It's probably ready and busy drying out.

5. Eat smaller portions of better quality meat. If you can afford meat, and if you can afford this book, then you're probably not starving.

6. With a selection or combination of salt, pepper, garlic, olive oil, soy sauce, mustard, chilli, paprika, lemon juice, a fresh herb and a cold drink, you can braai a great meal with any cut of meat.

7. The fire you make after you've braaied is called an atmosfire.

8. Life's too short to peel potatoes.